M·A·R·k 12™
Reading

W9-AAK-613

Activity Book

Volume III

Book Staff and Contributors

Kristen Kinney *Senior Content Specialist*
Amy Rauen *Instructional Designer*
David Shireman *Instructional Designer*
Michelle Iwaszuk *Instructional Designer*
Sarah Mastrianni *Writer*
Kandee Dyczko *Writer*
Tisha Ruibal *Writer*
Ben Justesen *Editor*
Suzanne Montazer *Senior Art Director*
Sasha Blanton *Senior Print Designer, Cover Designer*
Julie Jankowski *Print Designer*
Stephanie Shaw *Illustrator*
Chris Franklin *Illustrator*
Jayoung Cho *Illustrator*
Anja Hollinger *Project Manager*
Carrie Miller *Project Manager*

John Holdren *Senior Vice President for Content and Curriculum*
Maria Szalay *Senior Vice President for Product Development*
David Pelizzari *Vice President of Content and Curriculum*
Kim Barcas *Vice President of Creative Design*
Seth Herz *Director, Program Management*

Lisa Dimaio Iekel *Production Manager*
John G. Agnone *Director of Publications*

About K12 Inc.

K12 Inc., a technology-based education company, is the nation's leading provider of proprietary curriculum and online education programs to students in grades K–12. K[12] provides its curriculum and academic services to online schools, traditional classrooms, blended school programs, and directly to families. K12 Inc. also operates the K[12] International Academy, an accredited, diploma-granting online private school serving students world-wide. K[12]'s mission is to provide any child the curriculum and tools to maximize success in life, regardless of geographic, financial, or demographic circumstances. K12 Inc. is accredited by CITA. More information can be found at www.K12.com.

Copyright © 2009 K12 Inc. All rights reserved.

No part of this document may be reproduced or used in any form or by any means, graphic, electronic, or mechanical, including photocopying, recording, taping, and information retrieval systems, without the prior written permission of K12 Inc.

ISBN 978-1-60153-075-2

Printed by RR Donnelley, Willard, OH, USA, November 2014, Lot 112014

Contents

Long Vowels and Prefixes

Spelling /k/, /f/, /g/, & /j/ and Prefixes

/s/ & /sh/ and Suffixes

/oi/, /ou/, & /us/ and Suffixes

able/*ible* & /shun/ and Suffixes

Plurals & Two Vowels, Two Sounds and Base Words

Vowel Suffixes and Root Words

Contractions and Root Words

Compound Words and Root Words

Homophones and Root Words

/ə/ & Confusing Words and Root Words

Abbreviations and Root Words

Word Relationships and Root Words

Activity Book

Volume III

Finish the Sentence

Read each sentence aloud. Choose a word from the box to complete each sentence. Write the word on the line provided. Read the sentence again.

able	weigh	day	eight	steak
acorn	great	rain	gray	mail

Example: The chipmunk will eat the __acorn__ .

1. We played out in the _____ today.

2. She got a letter in the _____ .

3. The next _____ is going to be sunny and warm.

4. Tom's little brother is _____ years old.

5. We are having _____ for dinner today.

6. The sky is cloudy and _____ this morning.

7. John was sick, so he was not _____ to go to the play.

8. We all had a _____ time at the party.

9. He stepped on the scale to _____ himself.

© 2009 K12 Inc. All rights reserved.

Definitions

Draw a line from each word to the definition of that word. The first one has been done for you.

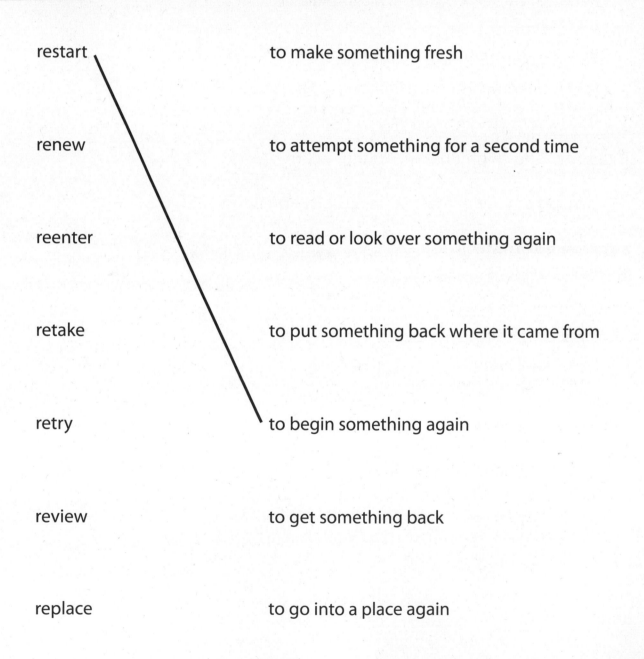

restart   to make something fresh

renew   to attempt something for a second time

reenter   to read or look over something again

retake   to put something back where it came from

retry   to begin something again

review   to get something back

replace   to go into a place again

© 2009 K12 Inc. All rights reserved.

Get Ready

🔲 Nouns name people, places, or things. Sometimes a noun is even an idea.
Here are some examples of nouns:

Persons: carpenter, parent, Mayor Ruiz

Places: library, New York, pond

Things: plate, Statue of Liberty, window

Ideas: freedom, sadness, liberty

🔲 Take a look at these two nouns:

city

Chicago

🔲 We call city a *common noun*. Common nouns tell about a general group or kind of person, place, or thing.

🔲 Chicago names a particular city. We call Chicago a *proper noun*. Proper nouns name a particular person, place, or thing. Proper nouns are capitalized.

Common Nouns	Proper Nouns
man	Mr. Brown
city	Jacksonville
team	The Lakers
state	Kansas
holiday	Thanksgiving Day
ocean	Pacific Ocean
author	E. B. White

© 2009 K12 Inc. All rights reserved.

Try It

Write each noun from the box in the correct column below the box.

| America | Arthur | banana | baseball | Boston | freedom |
| happiness | ice cream | Janice | justice | Martin | Vermont |

Person	**Place**	**Thing**	**Idea**
_____	_____	_____	_____
_____	_____	_____	_____
_____	_____	_____	_____

Underline the nouns in each sentence. Look carefully! Each sentence has two or more nouns.

1. Jennifer likes to play soccer.

2. The coach blows the whistle.

3. Bill saved his money for a new bike.

4. The bike shop is in Allentown.

5. Laura Ingalls Wilder wrote the book, *The Little House on the Prairie*.

6. Sandy has a dog named Rex.

7. Rex is a big, black Labrador retriever.

© 2009 K12 Inc. All rights reserved.

Name:

Sorting Words

Read each word in the box. Write each word from the box under the spelling pattern that is used to make the /ā/ sound in that word.

skate	play	freight	pain	pay	slate
weight	break	sail	steak	great	make
eight	stray	grain	train	tape	

/ā/ Spelled *ai*

_____

_____

_____

_____

/ā/ Spelled *eigh*

_____

_____

_____

_____

/ā/ Spelled *ea*

_____

_____

_____

_____

/ā/ Spelled *a-e*

_____

_____

_____

_____

/ā/ Spelled *ay*

_____

_____

_____

_____

© 2009 K12 Inc. All rights reserved.

Using Prefixes

Choose a word from the box to complete each sentence. Write the words on the lines provided.

undone	unsolvable	unaware	unbroken
unknown	uncommon	untied	unlikely

Example: It is __uncommon__ for rain to fall in the desert.

1. Jeremy left some of the problems _____ on his math worksheet.

2. It is _____ that we will get lost on the way home.

3. The hero _____ the ropes holding the prisoner.

4. The cup fell on the ground, but we were lucky that it was

   _____ .

5. Maria was _____ that there was a test today.

6. Pete's robot had been missing for days; its location was

   _____ .

7. The questions on this test are so difficult that they are almost

   _____ .

6

© 2009 K12 Inc. All rights reserved.

Backup Plan

It was a clear and bright afternoon in May. The sky was blue. The sun was shining. Lane could not sit still. "Only two more days and we'll be camping by the lake!" she called out to her father. "We've been planning this trip for months. It seemed like it would never arrive. Now it's finally here! Hiking in the morning! Fishing during the day!

© 2009 K12 Inc. All rights reserved.

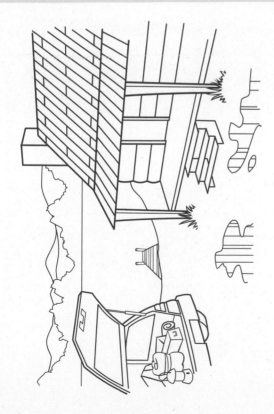

"Wow, Dad, you thought of everything. We may not be camping outside, but this camping trip is going to be great! We better get started setting up camp," Lane said. Then she ran over to give her father a big hug.

© 2009 K12 Inc. All rights reserved.

Campfires at night! We're going to have such a great time! I can't wait!"

"I'm excited, too," her father said. "We should check the weather report before we pack. It can get pretty chilly at night by the lake. We need to make sure we pack the right gear to keep us warm," he explained.

"I'll do that right now," Lane said. She walked over to the table to pick up the newspaper. "Oh, no!" she gasped. "The weather report in the newspaper says it's going to rain all weekend. We can't camp in the rain. Our trip is ruined." Then she folded her arms on the table and put her head down.

"It's our backup plan," he said. "We can't camp outdoors because it's raining, so we'll camp indoors instead. The fireplace will be our campfire. We'll use it to make our meals. We'll roast marshmallows before bed. We'll unroll our sleeping bags on the floor. We can't fish, but there's a fish tank inside. I can teach you about all of the fish swimming around. We'll sit out on the back porch at night and listen to the crickets and watch fireflies. In the morning, we can sit out on the back porch and listen to the birds. I can tell you the names of the ones I know. We can do all these things, and we can do them without getting wet!"

© 2009 K12 Inc. All rights reserved.

© 2009 K12 Inc. All rights reserved.

"Don't give up just yet, Lane. Sometimes the weather report changes. We won't know for sure until it's time to leave. Maybe we'll get lucky and have great weather. Let's pack and stick with the plan to head to the lake Friday morning."

Lane grew more excited with each passing day. She also grew more nervous that the weather would cause the trip to be put off for another time. On Friday morning, Lane jumped out of bed. She ran to the window. She began to frown as soon as she looked outside. The sky was gray and full of dark clouds. *So much for getting lucky and having great weather,* she thought. Lane went to find her father. She looked

© 2009 K12 Inc. All rights reserved.

© 2009 K12 Inc. All rights reserved.

all around the house with no luck. She was surprised to see him loading up the car. "We're still going camping?" she asked. "I didn't think you'd want to go in this weather. It looks like it could start raining at any minute."

"I think the trip will work out. It's cloudy now, but maybe the rain will stay away for a few more days," he answered, packing the last bag. "Let's get going. The sooner we head out, the sooner we start camping!"

Lane and her father climbed into the car and began their trip. As they drove, rain started to fall. First, just a few drops fell. Soon, the windows were covered with water. Lane turned to look at her

© 2009 K12 Inc. All rights reserved.

father. "It looks like the weather report was right. We should turn around now," she said. "The weather is not going to get any better. We'll have to take our trip some other time."

"Don't worry, Lane. We're not going to let a little rain mess up our weekend. I have a backup plan," her father said to her with a grin.

An hour later, Lane and her father pulled up to a cabin by the lake. Her father parked the car and began to unload their bags.

"What's this?" Lane asked. "We've never been here before."

© 2009 K12 Inc. All rights reserved.

Sounds at Night

Read the story below. In each blank space, fill in the /ē/ word from the box that makes the most sense for the story. The first word is filled in for you.

he	creak	creepy	happy	Steve	baby
thief	speak	asleep	sleepy	relief	

Steve was <u>asleep</u> in his bed. But then _____

woke up. He heard a sound. It was hard to describe the sound.

It was some kind of _____ . It came from

downstairs. Was there a _____ in the

house? _____ was a little bit scared. He

got out of bed. He walked past his _____

brother's room. He walked slowly downstairs. This was

_____ . He wanted to call out, but he was

too scared to _____ . Then Steve was at the

bottom of the stairs. He saw something move. It was the cat.

What a _____ ! The cat had been making the

sounds. Steve was _____ . But he was also

_____ , so he went back to bed.

© 2009 K12 Inc. All rights reserved.

Definitions

Choose three words from the box and write your own definition for each word. Next, write each word in a sentence. Make sure that the meaning of the word in your sentence matches your definition of the word.

prehistoric	prefix	preview	preheat	preschool	precut

Example:

Word: _precut_

Definition: _to cut something ahead of time, or before it is needed_

Sentence: _The art teacher precut some paper shapes for the_

next day's class.

Word: _____

Definition: _____

Sentence: _____

_____

Word: _____

Definition: _____

Sentence: _____

_____

Word: _____

Definition: _____

Sentence: _____

_____

© 2009 K12 Inc. All rights reserved.

Tic Tac Toe

Read the words below. Each word contains the /ē/ sound. Circle the five words in a row that rhyme. The row can be across, up, down, or diagonal.

tree	flea	bee	each	holly
three	see	glee	peach	jolly
sea	sheep	peep	teach	dear
dream	weep	thief	reach	Polly
steep	deep	Pete	beach	dolly

© 2009 K12 Inc. All rights reserved.

 **Work**

/ē/ and Prefix *sub–*

Crossword Puzzle

Read the clues to fill in the words in the crossword puzzle.

Hint: All of the answers use the prefix *sub–*.

Across

1. something that is very poorly made

2. a train that travels in a tunnel under the city

3. words that appear at the bottom of the screen in a movie

Down

4. a boat that can travel underneath the ocean

5. the area of the earth just below the arctic circle on a map

© 2009 K12 Inc. All rights reserved.

Ben found his favorite childhood book. Its corners were folded. Its pages were torn. Its cover was scratched. None of that mattered to Ben. As soon as he saw the book, he began to smile.

"I said I knew exactly what to do with you, and I do," he said, as he picked up the book. Ben walked down the hall and poked his head in his little sister's room. "Hi, Tess. Would you like me to read you a book?"

"I sure would!" Tess said, and she ran over to Ben and sat in his lap.

Just then, their mother walked by Tess's room. She looked in on Ben reading to Tess and smiled. She stood there until Ben finished reading to Tess.

doorway. "You know, I've read this book to you every night since you were a baby. I'm surprised you still like it."

"I love it! It's my favorite book. I'll never get tired of reading it!" he said.

Ben closed his eyes and listened to

his mother's voice. He pictured the

characters and all of their adventures

© 2009 K12 Inc. All rights reserved.

you, my little Ben," she said to him.

7

Old Friends, New Friends

"Ben, have you changed into your pajamas?" Ben's mother asked.

"Yes, Mommy," he answered.

"Have you brushed your teeth?"

© 2009 K12 Inc. All rights reserved.

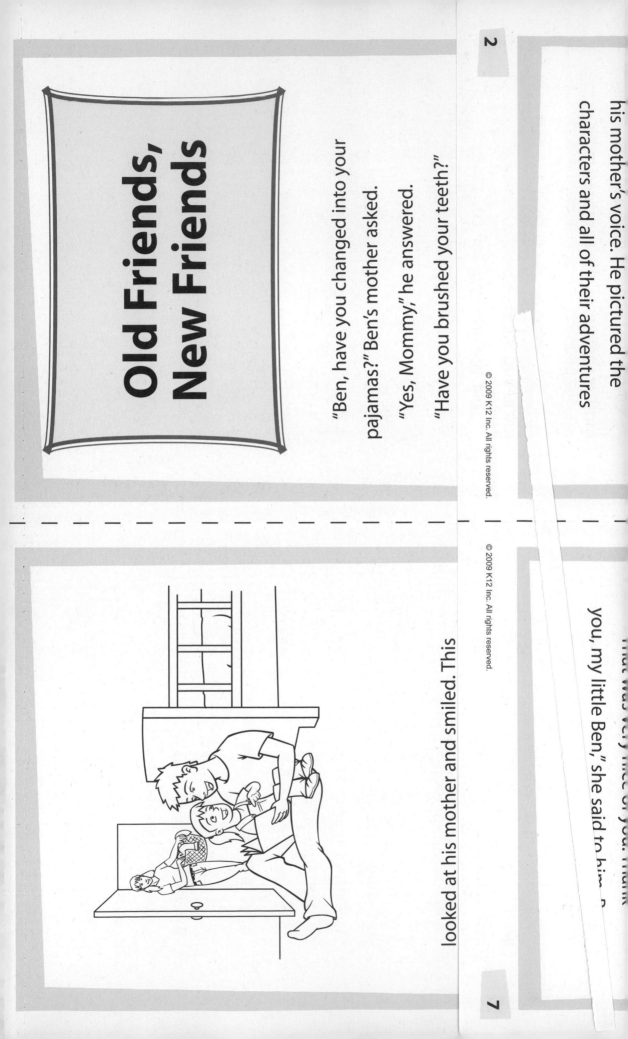

looked at his mother and smiled. This

as his mother read to him. Soon Ben drifted off to sleep.

"Good night, my little Ben," his mother whispered as she kissed his forehead. She pulled up his blanket and turned off his lamp. She walked over to the door and looked at her sleeping son one more time. Then she quietly closed his bedroom door.

Years later, Ben had outgrown his favorite book. He no longer asked his mother to tuck him in at night. He no longer asked her to read his favorite book to him before bed. He tossed the book aside to make room for a radio on his nightstand. He dropped the book on the floor as he carried toys to the closet. He stepped on it when he wasn't looking. He piled his clothes, shoes, and backpack on top of the book. As the

© 2009 K12 Inc. All rights reserved.

"I'm really sorry," Ben replied. "I know I've been busy. My room is a mess, but I should really take better care of you. I loved listening to your adventures when I was a kid. Just because I'm older now doesn't mean I should toss you aside. I know just what I'll do."

"Thank you, Ben! It makes us so happy to know you care," Miss Ladybug and Captain Cobweb said together. As soon as the words came from their mouths, the dream was over.

Ben opened his eyes to sunlight shining through his window. He threw off his blanket. He began cleaning his room at once. He put his football and baseball in a bin in his closet. He put all of his toy cars in a basket. He folded his clothes and put them away. At the bottom of a pile, under clothes and toys,

© 2009 K12 Inc. All rights reserved.

years passed by, Ben cared less and less for the old book that was now scratched and torn.

One night, Ben got ready for bed as he always did.

"Ben, did you brush your teeth?" his mother asked from another room.

"Yes, Mom. Good night," Ben replied.

"Good night, my little Ben," she said.

"Oh, Mom, I'm not a kid anymore. I'm too old for you to call me that."

"You'll always be my little Ben," his mother replied.

As he slept, Ben began to dream. In his dream, he was visited by two characters from his childhood book. "Miss Ladybug? Captain Cobweb? Is that you?" Ben asked. "I haven't seen you two in years," he said to his old friends.

© 2009 K12 Inc. All rights reserved.

"Yes, Ben, we know. That's the reason we're here. We miss seeing you each night before you go to bed, but we understand you're growing up. We know we're not your favorites anymore," Miss Ladybug said. Then she turned her head to hide her sadness.

"What really upsets us, though, is that you just don't take care of us anymore," Captain Cobweb explained. "You toss us on the floor. You pile other toys on top of us. You even walk over us. We're in pretty bad shape now. Have you seen us lately?" he asked.

"No, I guess I haven't," Ben said.

"Our pages are all folded and torn. Our cover is scratched. It's all very sad," Miss Ladybug said. Then she turned her head again.

© 2009 K12 Inc. All rights reserved.

Code Work

Name:

/ī/ and Prefix *dis–*

Finding Words

Read each sentence aloud. Underline each word that contains the /ī/ sound.

Hint: Each sentence has two or more /ī/ words.

Example: The <u>light</u> is too <u>bright</u>.

1. He tried to ride his bike.

2. The lightning had gone away by sunrise.

3. He did not mind if he was not on time.

4. We hiked past the sign on the highway.

5. The pine trees swayed in the mild night air.

6. The mice played while the cat was away.

7. Simon tried to tie his shoes.

© 2009 K12 Inc. All rights reserved.

Prefix Practice

Add the prefix *dis–* to each of the following words, and write the new words on the lines provided.

Example: agree   <u>disagree</u>

1. appoint _____
2. obey _____
3. appear _____
4. honest _____

5. please _____
6. honor _____
7. trust _____
8. like _____

Choose three of the words that you created above, and write each word in a sentence.

9. Word: _____

   Sentence: _____

10. Word: _____

   Sentence: _____

11. Word: _____

   Sentence: _____

© 2009 K12 Inc. All rights reserved.

Get Ready

- When a noun names **only one** person, place, or thing, the noun is singular. When a noun names **more than one** person, place, or thing, the noun is plural.

Singular	Plural
scooter	scooters
helmet	helmets
injury	injuries

- **Regular Plural Nouns:** To make most singular nouns plural, add *–s* or *–es* to the end. These are called regular plural forms.

Singular	Plural
head	heads

Add *–es* to form the plural of nouns that end in *s, x, z, ch,* or *sh.*

Singular	Plural
moss	mosses
wish	wishes

Change the *y* to *i* and then add *–es* to form the plural of nouns that end in *y* after a consonant.

Singular	Plural
strawberry	strawberries
ally	allies

- **Irregular Plural Nouns:** Some nouns have irregular plurals. You probably know many of these already. You need to memorize the irregular plurals.

Singular	Plural
child	children
tooth	teeth

© 2009 K12 Inc. All rights reserved.

Try It

Write the plural form of each noun.

1. peach _____
2. cherry _____
3. boy _____
4. fox _____
5. child _____
6. kid _____

7. berry _____
8. box _____
9. ferry _____
10. girl _____
11. goose _____
12. cup _____

Complete each sentence with the plural form of each word in parentheses.

13. I have a lot of _____ (friend), so I go to a lot of

    _____ (party).

14. Can you please pass the _____ (berry)?

15. I have two red _____ (sock). I need to put them on my

    _____ (foot).

16. Bill and Artie are _____ (teammate). Their

    _____ (uniform) match.

17. I need _____ (apple), _____ (cracker), and
    juice from the store.

18. Farmers once used _____ (ox) to plow this field.

© 2009 K12 Inc. All rights reserved.

Finish the Job

Read each sentence. Choose a word from the box to complete each sentence. Read each sentence again.

supply	child	bike	fight
climb	lie	sunlight	why

Example: The store had a small __supply__ of shoes.

1. Rob was mad after his _____ with his sister.

2. The _____ wanted to play at the park.

3. Cats can _____ very tall trees.

4. The summer _____ is very hot.

5. I don't know _____ the phone isn't working.

6. Jin told a _____ and got in trouble.

7. I like to ride my _____ near the beach.

© 2009 K12 Inc. All rights reserved.

Prefix Practice

Add the prefix _mis–_ to each of the words below and write the new word on the line provided.

Example: judge ___misjudge___

1. print _____

2. spell _____

3. lead _____

4. fortune _____

5. read _____

6. behave _____

7. place _____

8. lay _____

Choose three of the words that you created above and write each word in a sentence on the lines provided below.

9. Word: _____

Sentence: _____

_____

10. Word: _____

Sentence: _____

_____

11. Word: _____

Sentence: _____

_____

© 2009 K12 Inc. All rights reserved.

The Dive

Franklin packed his sunscreen and a towel. He took one last bite of his lunch. Then he walked out the door. He hurried down the stairs of his building and jumped on his bike. He waved to his neighbors sitting outside. They smiled and waved back. They knew exactly where Franklin was going in such a hurry. Franklin pedaled as fast as he could until he arrived at the

© 2009 K12 Inc. All rights reserved.

"Thanks, Janet. You really helped me today," Franklin said. "I came to the pool afraid to dive. Now I don't want to do anything else but dive!"

Franklin dove until it was time to leave. Then he and Janet climbed out of the pool and dried off. They walked over to their bikes and made plans to meet tomorrow. "Same time, same place?" Franklin asked.

"Same time, same place," Janet replied. "Just make sure you share the diving board tomorrow," she joked. Then they hopped on their bikes and rode home.

© 2009 K12 Inc. All rights reserved.

© 2009 K12 Inc. All rights reserved.

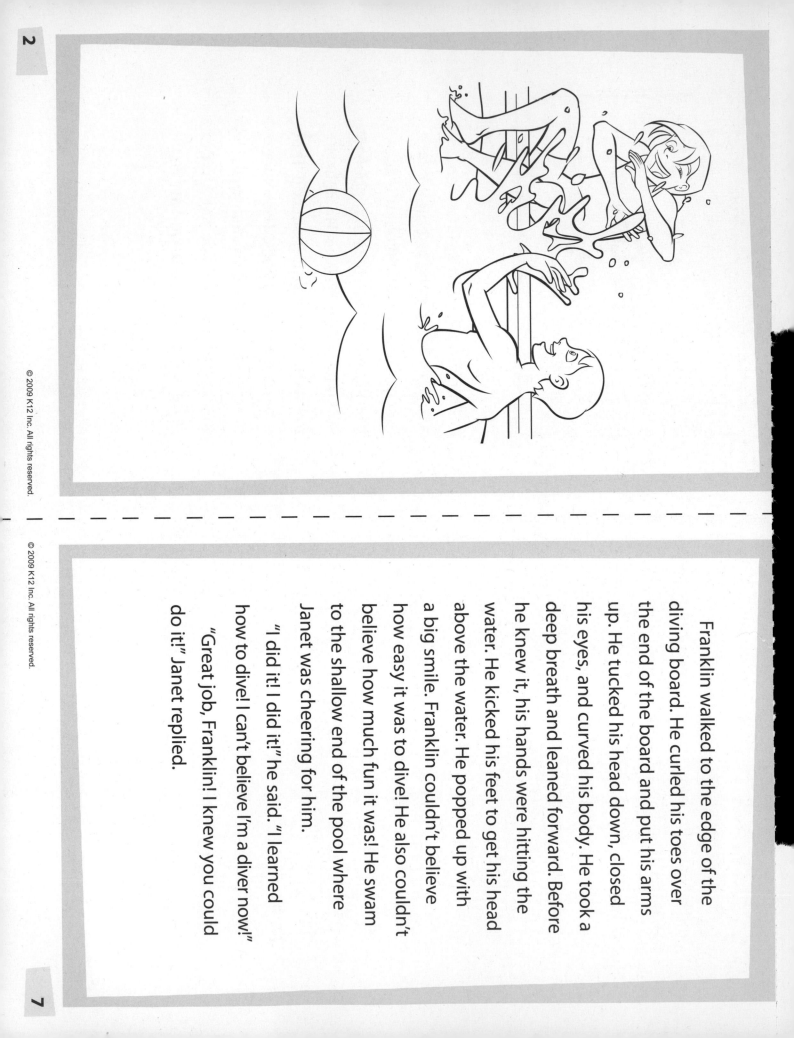

© 2009 K12 Inc. All rights reserved.

Franklin walked to the edge of the diving board. He curled his toes over the end of the board and put his arms up. He tucked his head down, closed his eyes, and curved his body. He took a deep breath and leaned forward. Before he knew it, his hands were hitting the water. He kicked his feet to get his head above the water. He popped up with a big smile. Franklin couldn't believe how easy it was to dive! He also couldn't believe how much fun it was! He swam to the shallow end of the pool where Janet was cheering for him.

"I did it! I did it!" he said. "I learned how to dive! I can't believe I'm a diver now!"

"Great job, Franklin! I knew you could do it!" Janet replied.

neighborhood pool. His friend Janet was already there waiting. She had her bag over her shoulder, and her bike was leaning against the wall. "Hi, Franklin. Ready for another day at the pool?" she asked.

"I sure am!" he said. "Summer is the best time of year, because we can swim every day!"

Franklin and Janet locked up their bikes and grabbed their bags. They walked over to the pool and set down their stuff. Then they walked into the shallow end and started swimming around. They splashed each other, slid down the waterslide, and played a few games. Soon, Janet stepped out of the

© 2009 K12 Inc. All rights reserved.

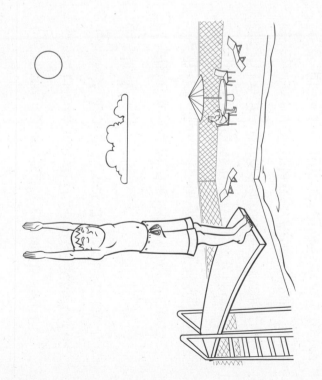

"You can do it, Franklin. Just remember everything we've worked on today," Janet said. She climbed back down from the diving board and walked over to the shallow end to watch Franklin's dive.

9 K12 Inc. All rights reserved.

© 2009 K12 Inc. All rights reserved.

pool and walked over to the diving board. She climbed up the stairs and dove into the deep end. After her dive, she swam over to Franklin. "We come here every day, and I've never seen you dive. You like to swim and you're good at it. Don't you want to dive?" she asked.

"I never learned how to dive, so I'm a little scared to try," he answered. "It looks like fun, but I just can't bring myself to do it."

"I can teach you if you want," Janet said. "I used to be scared to dive, too. It's really easy once you've learned how to do it. As much as you like swimming, I'm sure you'll love diving!"

© 2009 K12 Inc. All rights reserved.

"All right, Janet, that sounds like a plan. Even though I'm a little scared, I'm excited, too! Let's get started!" Franklin replied.

For the rest of the afternoon, Janet taught Franklin how to dive. First, she taught him how to dive from the side of the pool. With each dive, Franklin seemed more relaxed. After diving from the side a few times, he was ready to try the diving board. He and Janet climbed to the top of the board and looked down. Janet could tell Franklin was a bit nervous, so she told him to jump and curl into ... they both laughed at the big splash he made. Franklin climbed back to the top of the diving board and looked at Janet. "I think I'm ready to try," he said.

Finding Words

Read each sentence aloud. Circle each word that contains the /ō/ sound.
Hint: Each sentence has two or more /ō/ words.

Example: The (snow) is very (cold.)

1. His coach sent a note home to his parents.

2. The boat sailed across the ocean.

3. He did not want to let go of the rope.

4. John stubbed his big toe on the old bed.

5. The only thing I know how to make is toast.

6. The doe heard me when my foot kicked a stone.

© 2009 K12 Inc. All rights reserved.

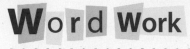

Name:

/ō/ and Prefix *in–*

Prefix Crossword

Read the clues, then fill in the words in the crossword.
Hint: All of the answers use the prefix *in–*.

Across

1. not enough of something

2. not correct

3. not capable

4. not finished yet

Down

5. no set limit to the number of something

2. a very lazy person

6. not accurate

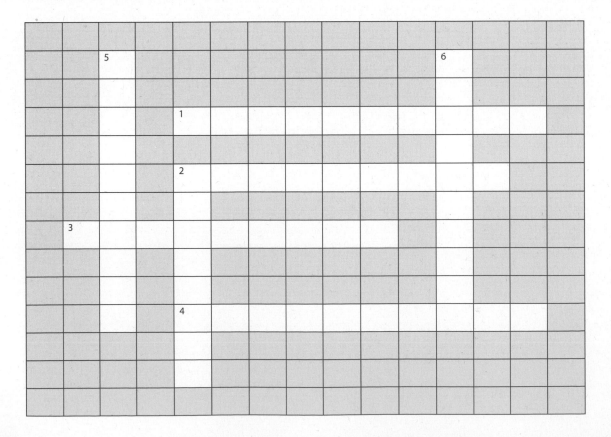

© 2009 K12 Inc. All rights reserved.

/ō/ and Prefix *bi–*

Place the Sound

Read each word aloud. Write the words in the correct column below.
The first word in each column has been done for you.

cold	doe	hoe	grow
toe	boat	row	both
hold	more	most	foe

/ō/ Sound in the Middle of the Word

/ō/ Sound at the End of the Word

cold _____

toe _____

_____ _____

_____ _____

_____ _____

_____ _____

© 2009 K12 Inc. All rights reserved.

Complete the Sentence

The prefix *bi–* means "two." Read the words and their definitions. Use the words to complete the sentences.

Word	Meaning
bicycle	a vehicle with two wheels, one behind the other
biannual	happening two times a year
biweekly	happening every other week
bimonthly	happening every other month
biplane	an airplane with two sets of wings, one above the other
binoculars	a tool for seeing faraway objects

1. We make _____ visits to the dentist; in other words, we go every six months.

2. Use the _____ to see if you can spot any wildlife in the distance.

3. Darrell buys a new comic book _____ , so he buys 26 comic books each year.

4. When I was little, I rode a tricycle. But when I got older, I learned to ride a _____ .

5. Our club meets _____ ; we have six meetings a year.

6. At the air show, we saw an old-fashioned airplane with two sets of wings; it was called a _____ .

© 2009 K12 Inc. All rights reserved.

Friendship Cookies

Oh, great, Joan thought, as she stepped onto the bus after a day at camp. *Why did I have to stand around talking to my friends? I knew this would happen if I didn't hurry and get to the bus.* She scanned the seats one last time. Sure enough, there was only one seat left. Joan began the slow walk to the back of the bus. *I don't want to sit next to*

© 2009 K12 Inc. All rights reserved.

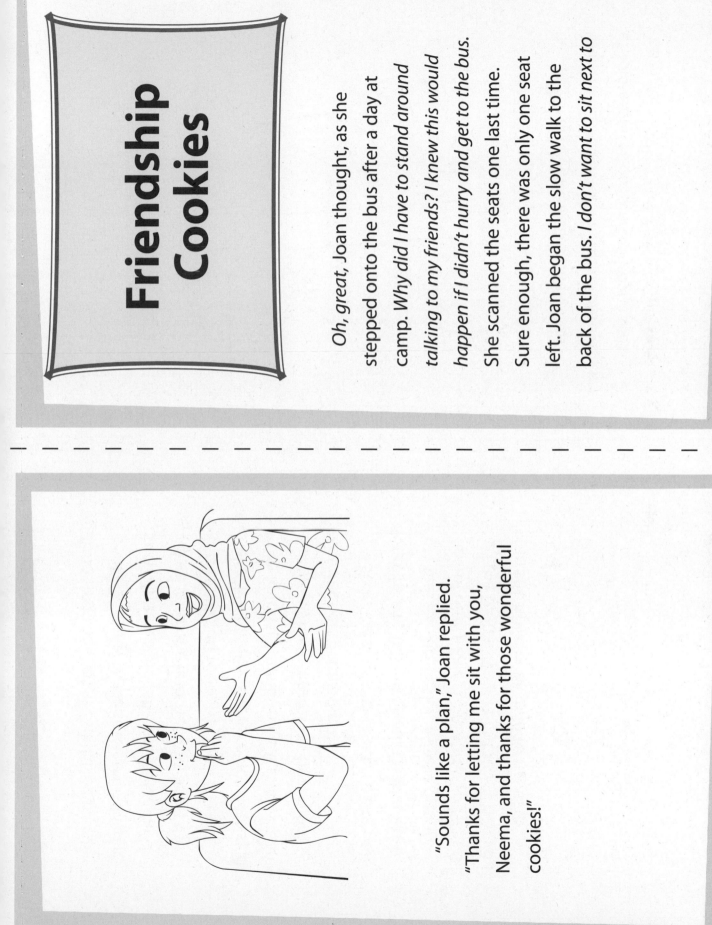

"Sounds like a plan," Joan replied. "Thanks for letting me sit with you, Neema, and thanks for those wonderful cookies!"

© 2009 K12 Inc. All rights reserved.

© 2009 K12 Inc. All rights reserved.

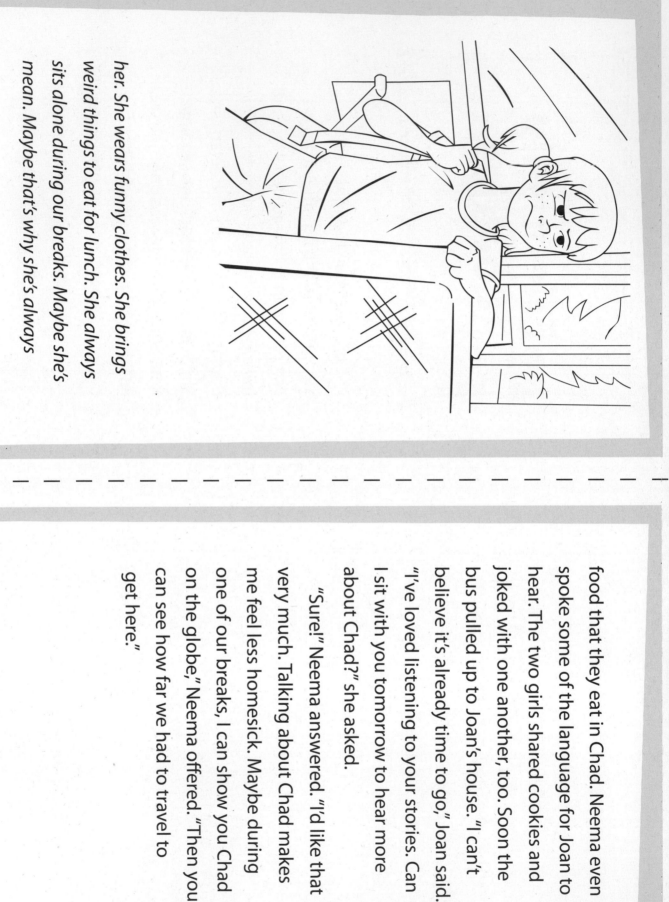

her. She wears funny clothes. She brings weird things to eat for lunch. She always sits alone during our breaks. Maybe she's mean. Maybe that's why she's always

© 2009 K12 Inc. All rights reserved.

food that they eat in Chad. Neema even spoke some of the language for Joan to hear. The two girls shared cookies and joked with one another, too. Soon the bus pulled up to Joan's house. "I can't believe it's already time to go," Joan said. "I've loved listening to your stories. Can I sit with you tomorrow to hear more about Chad?" she asked.

"Sure!" Neema answered. "I'd like that very much. Talking about Chad makes me feel less homesick. Maybe during one of our breaks, I can show you Chad on the globe," Neema offered. "Then you can see how far we had to travel to get here."

alone, Joan thought. She got to the last row and sat down. She didn't look over at the girl seated next to her. Joan tried not to sit too close to her.

"Hi. My name is Neema," the girl said with a smile. Joan noticed that the girl spoke differently from the other students.

"I'm Joan," Joan replied, without looking up. Just then, Joan's stomach growled.

"I have some leftover cookies from lunch. Would you like some?" Neema offered.

"Thanks. That's really nice of you," Joan replied. She finally looked up at the girl sitting next to her.

© 2009 K12 Inc. All rights reserved.

For the first time, Joan thought about how she had been acting towards Neema. "Neema, I would like to say I'm sorry. I never wanted to sit next to you because you don't dress like the rest of the kids at camp and you don't eat the same kind of food we eat," Joan explained. "I understand now that I was wrong. I shouldn't have stayed away from you for those reasons. I'd love to learn more about Chad."

Neema was happy that Joan wanted to know more. She spent the rest of the bus ride telling Joan about Chad. She told her stories about growing up there. She told her about the family and friends she left behind. She described the clothes that people wear and the

© 2009 K12 Inc. All rights reserved.

Neema reached into her backpack and pulled out a small bag of cookies. "Here you go," she said. "These are my favorite cookies. I hope you like them."

Joan opened the bag and peeked inside. "These don't look like any cookies I've ever had before," she said. She reached into the bag and pulled out a small cookie. Joan took a bite as she listened to Neema.

"My mom makes these for my family. These are the cookies we ate in our country before we moved here," Neema explained. "I love eating them because they remind me of home."

"I didn't know you were from a different country. Where are you from?" Joan asked. She had never met someone

from a different country before. Joan moved a little closer to Neema so she could hear her better. Then she took another bite of cookie.

"My family is from Chad. It's a country in Africa. We moved here a few months ago," Neema said. Joan could tell Neema was sad about moving.

"That's neat that you are from another country," Joan replied. "What's it like there?"

"It is different in Chad. Everyone wears clothes like mine. They eat the kind of food I eat. They speak the language I speak at home. I miss it very much. All of my friends are there. I think about them every day, especially when I have to sit alone," Neema said.

Name:

Spelling Search

Read each word in the chart below. Then mark each word as follows:

• Circle each word in which /ū/ is spelled *u-e* (as in cube).
• Cross out each word in which /ū/ is spelled *ue* (as in argue).
• Draw a box around each word in which /ū/ is spelled by the letter *u* alone (as in music).

One example of each spelling has been completed for you.

cube	music	hue	argue	mule
cupid	use	pupil	rescue	fumes
menu	using	bugle	humid	human
fuel	cute	value	unite	unicorn
mute	unit	continue	museum	cue

© 2009 K12 Inc. All rights reserved.

Prefix Practice

Add the prefix *semi–* to each of the words below, and write the new word on the line provided.

Example: final   <u>semifinal</u>

1. pro _____
2. circle _____
3. private _____
4. formal _____

5. rigid _____
6. skilled _____
7. conductor _____
8. gloss _____

Choose three of the words that you created above and use each word in a sentence below. Write the words and sentences on the lines provided.

Word: _____

Sentence: _____

_____

Word: _____

Sentence: _____

_____

Word: _____

Sentence: _____

_____

© 2009 K12 Inc. All rights reserved.

Get Ready

- A noun identifies a person, a place, or a thing. A noun can be *singular* (one book) or *plural* (two books). Singular means one. Plural means more than one.

- **Regular Plural Nouns:** Most of the time, you simply add an *–s* to a noun to make it plural. If the noun ends in *s, x, z, ch,* or *sh,* however, you have to add *–es.*

- **Irregular Plural Nouns:** Sometimes, the spelling of a noun has to change in order to become plural. Many of these words you already know:

Singular	Irregular Plural
child	children
goose	geese
tooth	teeth
foot	feet

© 2009 K12 Inc. All rights reserved.

Try It – Singular or Plural?

Look at each word. If the word is singular, write an "S" on the line provided next to the word. If the word is plural, write a "P" on the line provided next to the word.

1. day _____   5. bricks _____

2. mice _____   6. tooth _____

3. cow _____   7. feet _____

4. boxes _____   8. plant _____

Writing Plural Forms

Write the plural form of each noun below on the line provided.

9. bench _____   13. grape _____

10. mouse _____   14. tooth _____

11. wish _____   15. elephant _____

12. couch _____   16. brick _____

© 2009 K12 Inc. All rights reserved.

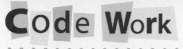
Sorting Vowel Spellings

Read each word in the box below. Write each word on the line provided under the spelling pattern used to make the /ū/ sound in that word.

| humor | uniform | cute | rescue | cube | argue |
| continue | human | hue | mute | music | use |

/ū/ Spelled *u-e*	**/ū/ Spelled *ue***	**/ū/ Spelled *u***
_____	_____	_____
_____	_____	_____
_____	_____	_____
_____	_____	_____

Choose three words from the box above. Write each word in a sentence below on the lines provided.

Sentences:

1. _____

_____

2. _____

_____

3. _____

_____

© 2009 K12 Inc. All rights reserved.

Definitions

Draw a line from each word on the left to the definition of that word on the right.

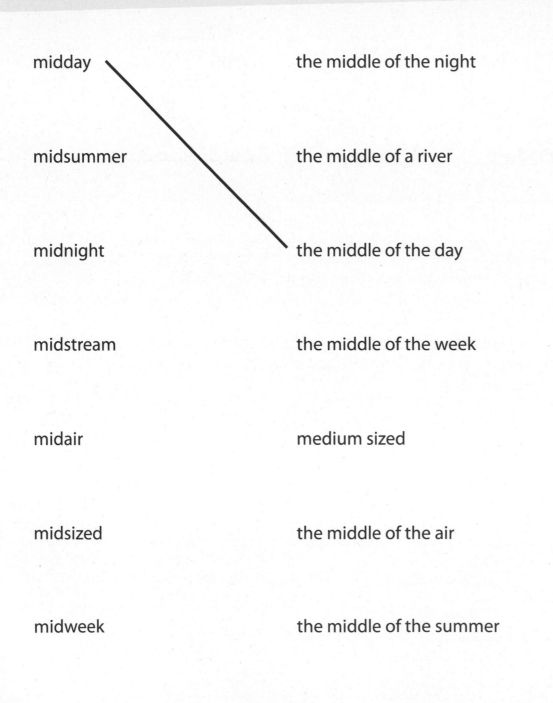

midday   the middle of the night

midsummer   the middle of a river

midnight   the middle of the day

midstream   the middle of the week

midair   medium sized

midsized   the middle of the air

midweek   the middle of the summer

© 2009 K12 Inc. All rights reserved.

Return to Roommates

"You can't do that!" Wade yelled at his brother.

"Oh, yes I can!" Saul yelled back.

"No, you can't! That's final!" Wade shouted.

"Boys, what's going on here?" their mom asked. "I've never seen you like this. You've been arguing for days. Something must be done. I think I'll move one of you to the guest room for

© 2009 K12 Inc. All rights reserved.

take a few weeks before you two started getting along again. Instead, it only took a few days!" With that, Wade and Saul headed upstairs, this time, to the same room.

© 2009 K12 Inc. All rights reserved.

a while. That way you two won't have to share a room."

"Thanks, Mom. I don't think I can spend one more day in the same room as Wade. I just can't do it," Saul stated.

"Hey, it's no picnic sharing a room with you, either," Wade shot back.

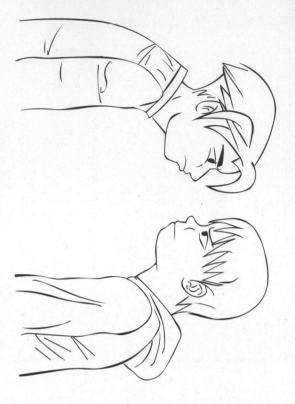

© 2009 K12 Inc. All rights reserved.

---

seem to be getting along again," Mom pointed out.

"I think maybe we just needed some time to realize how much we like each other," Saul said. "It's nice to have someone to talk to all the time. It's also nice to have someone to wake me up in the morning!"

"I agree. It's nice to have someone to help me work on my soccer skills. It's also nice to have someone to talk to until we fall asleep," Wade added. "I guess I can try to keep my stuff on my side of the room."

"Maybe I can turn down my music," Saul offered.

"I think that sounds great, boys. You know what's funny? I thought it would

© 2009 K12 Inc. All rights reserved.

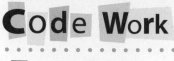

/ oo / and Prefix fore–

The Big Meal

Read the story below. On the lines provided, fill in the word with the / oo / sound from the box that makes the most sense for the story. The first word is done for you.

cool	rude	true	Bamboo	smooth
spoon	food	group	blue	
included	too	soup	room	

Steve was going out to eat with a __group__ of his friends.

They were going to the _____ Café. That was a place

that Steve liked a lot. The waiters were _____, but the

_____ was good. He ordered the tomato _____.

It came in a really big _____ bowl with a really big

_____. Steve's friends said it would be _____

big for him. The soup was _____ and creamy, and it

was really hot. But after it got _____, it was very good.

The meal also _____ crackers and some fruit. It was

_____ that he got really full, but he did finish the whole

meal. Now he needed to go back to his _____ for a nap!

© 2009 K12 Inc. All rights reserved.

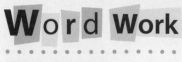

/oo/ and Prefix _fore–_

Using Prefixes

Choose a word from the box to complete each sentence below. Write the words on the lines provided.

forecast	foresee	forewarn	forefathers
forearms	foreleg	foreground	foreshadowed

Example: The horse hurt his right ___foreleg___ and started limping.

1. I could _____ that I would find some coins in the washing machine.

2. The painting showed some apples in the _____ .

3. Hundreds of years ago, my _____ bought this land for my family.

4. The weather _____ is for lots of sunshine next week.

5. I tried to _____ Jeremy that he would get hurt climbing the tree.

6. Trying to hang on the monkey bars for so long made my _____ sore.

7. In the movie, the black birds that flew through the sky _____ tragedy.

© 2009 K12 Inc. All rights reserved.

Get Ready

▪ Nouns (persons, places, or things) can be singular or plural. The possessive form of a singular noun shows possession or ownership. The apostrophe (') is a sign of a possessive noun. To create the possessive form of a singular noun, add *'s* to the end of the noun, even when the noun already ends with an *s*.

Singular	Possessive
teacher	teacher's
Martin	Martin's
Charles	Charles's

▪ Look at the following examples. Notice that the *'s* makes it easier to show possession or ownership

the doll of Becky	Becky's doll
the bone of the dog	the dog's bone
the wish made by Chris	Chris's wish

Try It

Underline the singular possessive nouns in each sentence below.

1. I have Julie's brush in my bag.

2. We are going to Thomas's party at noon.

3. Vermont's state flower is red clover.

4. The house's front door is painted red.

© 2009 K12 Inc. All rights reserved.

Rewrite the following phrases by using singular possessive nouns.

5. the tennis racket that Mary owns _____

6. the leaves of the tree _____

7. the banana for the monkey _____

8. the watch that belongs to Dad _____

Write the noun's possessive form to complete each sentence below.

9. Mabel: _____ sister is in 9th grade.

10. cat: I can't find the _____ toy mouse.

11. Avery: What did _____ letter say?

12. cup: The _____ handle is cracked.

13. friend: My _____ mom works at the hospital.

Draw a line from each noun to that noun's possessive form.

14. the boy   Maine's

15. Ella   Ella's

16. Maine   the ape's

17. the lake   the boy's

18. Jake   the lake's

19. the ape   Jake's

© 2009 K12 Inc. All rights reserved.

Name:

/ōō/ and Prefix *under–*

Finding /ōō/ Words

Read each sentence aloud. Underline each word that contains the /ōō/ sound.

Hint: Each sentence has more than one /ōō/ word. The first one has been done for you.

1. There is a <u>rumor</u> that John's family is putting in a <u>pool</u>.

2. I put ice in the cooler so that the tuna would keep cool.

3. I looked like a fool when I sat in the glue.

4. Her room was too messy, so she could not find her flute.

5. If you break the rules, there will be trouble.

6. The roof over the deck helps keep it cool in the sun.

7. On the first night of June, look for the full moon.

8. At the zoo, we saw a baboon, a goose, and a kangaroo.

9. Is it true that you painted your bedroom blue and green?

10. It is rude to hang your spoon from your nose in a restaurant.

© 2009 K12 Inc. All rights reserved.

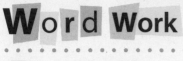

Prefix Practice

Add the prefix *under–* to each of the following words, and then write the new words on the lines provided.

Example: fed ___underfed___

1. age _____
2. estimate _____
3. ground _____
4. done _____

5. pass _____
6. sea _____
7. sized _____
8. line _____

Choose three of the words that you created above, and write each word in a sentence below. Write your words and sentences on the lines provided.

Word: _____

Sentence: _____

_____

Word: _____

Sentence: _____

_____

Word: _____

Sentence: _____

_____

© 2009 K12 Inc. All rights reserved.

A Birthday Surprise

Sue hung up the phone and plopped down on her stool. Her father could tell by the look on her face that the news was not good. "That was Julie. She's busy, too. Some birthday this will be," Sue said, with a look of gloom. "None of my friends can come to my party next week. We can't have a party with no guests. I guess I'll just hang out in my room that day."

Sue spent the rest of the afternoon swimming and enjoying her party with her friends. Her father and aunt watched as she talked and laughed for hours. "I guess the surprise was worth it," Dad told Sue's aunt. "I hated seeing her sad all week, but it looks like we made the right choice."

"I agree. It would have been a shame to spoil the surprise. I guess we better start thinking about next year's party. It's going to take hard work to beat this one!" her aunt said. Then they looked at each other and laughed.

© 2009 K12 Inc. All rights reserved.

© 2009 K12 Inc. All rights reserved.

© 2009 K12 Inc. All rights reserved.

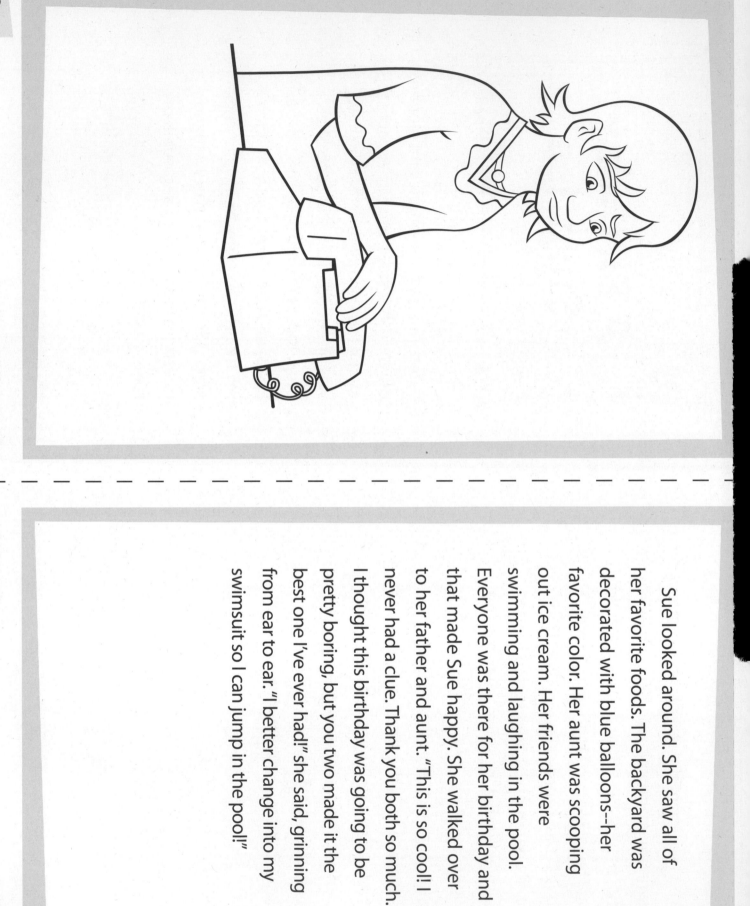

© 2009 K12 Inc. All rights reserved.

Sue looked around. She saw all of her favorite foods. The backyard was decorated with blue balloons--her favorite color. Her aunt was scooping out ice cream. Her friends were swimming and laughing in the pool. Everyone was there for her birthday and that made Sue happy. She walked over to her father and aunt. "This is so cool! I never had a clue. Thank you both so much. I thought this birthday was going to be pretty boring, but you two made it the best one I've ever had!" she said, grinning from ear to ear. "I better change into my swimsuit so I can jump in the pool!"

"I'm sorry that all of your friends are busy. It is June. Everyone is probably busy with summer activities," Dad said.

"Don't worry. I won't let you hang out in your room on your birthday. We can go over to your aunt's house. I'm sure she'd love to see you that day. We can eat cake and ice cream and watch any movie you want. We can also swim in her pool, if you feel like it."

"That sounds like a good plan. It'll be nice to see her," Sue said. She tried her hardest to look cheerful, but her father knew she was unhappy. He also knew that she would have more fun on her birthday than she realized.

"They did. They all had plans to come here. Your aunt and I have had this party planned for quite some time now," Dad explained.

"It was hard to keep the secret, but we knew we had to do it. We knew if we told you the truth, we would spoil the surprise," her aunt said.

© 2009 K12 Inc. All rights reserved.

© 2009 K12 Inc. All rights reserved.

Sue was sad all week. She had been looking forward to her party, but now it wasn't going to happen. She tried to stay busy and keep her mind off of her birthday. She spent the days riding her skateboard. At night, she played her flute. She usually enjoyed doing both of those things, but even they didn't make her happy. Her father tried to cheer her up, but her mood did not improve. When her birthday finally arrived, he gave her a new skateboard. "Thanks, Dad! I know you've been trying to cheer me up all week. I think it's time I snap out of it. I'm going to try to be happy again," Sue told her father.

"I'm glad to hear that, Sue. I know your aunt wants to see you happy on your birthday. I told her we'd get to her house by noon. We should head over there. Don't forget to grab your swimsuit," Dad said.

When Sue and Dad arrived at her aunt's house, the door was open. They walked inside the house. "I'm out by the pool!" Sue's aunt shouted from the backyard. Sue and her father walked out the back door.

"Surprise!" everyone shouted as Sue stepped outside. "Happy birthday, Sue!"

"Wow!" Sue said, with a look of shock. "How did you get all of my friends here?" Sue asked. "I thought they all had plans."

© 2009 K12 Inc. All rights reserved.

© 2009 K12 Inc. All rights reserved.

Mystery Words

Choose a word from the box to match each clue below. Write each word in the second column on the lines provided. Read aloud each word that you write, and listen for the /o͞o/ sound.

book	barefoot	took	wood	good
cook	football	notebook	woof	stood

Clue   Word

1. something you read _____

2. wearing no shoes _____

3. past tense of stand _____

4. you burn this in a fireplace _____

5. opposite of bad _____

6. what you do in a kitchen _____

7. a sport played outside _____

8. you write in this _____

9. sound a dog makes _____

10. past tense of take _____

© 2009 K12 Inc. All rights reserved.

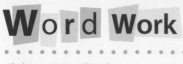

Using the Prefix *de–*

The prefix *de–* means "to reverse or to remove." Choose a word from the box to match each phrase below. Write each word in the second column.

| dethrone | dehydrate | decode |
| defrost | debone | deforest |

Phrase	**Word**
1. to remove frost by thawing	_____
2. to remove water or moisture from something	_____
3. to remove a code	_____
4. to remove from the throne	_____
5. to remove bones from meat	_____
6. to remove trees from a forest	_____

Choose four words from the box above. On the lines provided below, write sentences using each word that you chose.

7. _____

_____

8. _____

_____

9. _____

_____

10. _____

_____

© 2009 K12 Inc. All rights reserved.

Sentence Completion

Choose a word from the box to complete each sentence below. Write the words on the lines provided. Then read each word aloud.

could	barefoot	would	good	push
pull	cook	put	took	should

1. You _____ eat lots of fruits and vegetables.

2. My little sister thinks it is funny to _____ my hair, but I do not like it.

3. Will you please _____ the salt and pepper over to me?

4. He _____ not hear the music, so he turned it up louder.

5. They took off their shoes to walk _____ on the soft grass.

6. I am going to _____ dinner for my family tonight.

7. It _____ him all day to clean his room.

8. I thought it was a _____ show, but my friend did not like it.

9. Did you _____ away the broom after you used it to sweep the kitchen?

10. _____ you like to hear me play a song on the flute?

© 2009 K12 Inc. All rights reserved.

Using the Prefix *uni–*

The prefix *uni–* means "one." Choose a word from the box to match each phrase below. Write each word on the lines provided in the second column.
Hint: One word will be used more than once.

| uniped | uniform | unicolored | unicycle |

Phrase	**Word**

1. one standard set of clothing worn by many
   people in a group   _____

2. a one-wheeled vehicle   _____

3. having only one leg or foot   _____

4. having one standard way of doing something   _____

5. having only one color   _____

Choose two words from the box above. On the lines provided below,
write sentences using each word that you chose.

6. _____

   _____

7. _____

   _____

© 2009 K12 Inc. All rights reserved.

The Yearbook Scare

The final draft of the drama club yearbook was complete. Mac had stayed behind after play rehearsal to add the finishing touches. He had to turn it in the next day. All of the stories had been written and revised. All of the pictures had been taken and captioned. All of the due dates had been met. Now all that was left to do was hand over the draft to Mr. Shaw, the play director.

© 2009 K12 Inc. All rights reserved.

"Sorry I can't share in your good mood," Mac replied. "I'm looking for the final draft of the yearbook. I still can't believe I lost it."

"That's because you didn't lose it!" Nell said. Then she reached into her bag. She pulled out the draft and handed it to Mac. "Lucas and I took it yesterday. We wanted to write a thank-you letter, on behalf of all the members of the drama club, for all of your hard work."

"We included it with the final draft. It'll be the first page in the yearbook," Lucas added.

"Thank you both. That's really nice of you," Mac said. "I guess it was worth the panic!" he said, and opened the draft to read the letter.

© 2009 K12 Inc. All rights reserved.

© 2009 K12 Inc. All rights reserved.

© 2009 K12 Inc. All rights reserved.

"Don't panic, Mac. I'm sure we'll find it. It must be here somewhere," Mr. Shaw said. He began looking around the room.

Mac looked around the room, too. He looked for the draft in every desk. He looked for it on the floor. He even looked in the trash can. "I'm really sorry," Mac said sadly. "I know you had to take the draft to get printed today. Now the yearbooks will be late. Everyone in the drama club is going to be upset. This is horrible and it's all my fault."

Just then, Nell and Lucas hurried into the room. "Well, we thought we would beat you here this morning. I guess we were wrong," Lucas said. He and Nell were smiling, but Mac was in no mood to smile.

He would take it to the printing company tomorrow. Mac was glad that all the hard work was done. He flipped through the pages one more time. He wanted to make sure each play that the club had performed this year was included. Then he carefully slid the draft into his backpack. Mac couldn't wait to pass it off to Mr. Shaw first thing in the morning. Just then, Nell and Lucas walked into the rehearsal room. Nell wrote stories for the yearbook and Lucas took pictures.

"Hi, Mac. Was that your notebook we saw outside in the hall?" Nell asked.

"I wouldn't be surprised," Mac responded. "With all these last-minute details for the yearbook, I've been kind

© 2009 K12 Inc. All rights reserved.

to shake it. Mr. Shaw saw the look of panic on Mac's face as he shook his backpack.

"Is everything all right, Mac?" he asked. "You look worried."

"I know I put it in here yesterday. Now it's not here. The final draft of the yearbook is missing!" Mac gasped.

© 2009 K12 Inc. All rights reserved.

of forgetful with everything else. I'll go check," Mac walked out into the hallway.

He saw his notebook on the floor. As he reached down to pick it up, Nell and Lucas sped past him.

"See you later, Mac," Lucas called out, without looking back.

I wonder where they're going in such a hurry, Mac thought. He walked back inside the room. He put the notebook in his backpack. Then Mac went home.

Mac was unable to sleep that night. All he could do was think about the yearbook. He pictured each page in his mind. He made mental changes to some of the pages, but he always changed his mind back. *The yearbook is great the way it is. I should just leave it alone*, Mac

thought. Then he finally drifted off to sleep.

Mac woke up early the next morning. He quickly ate his breakfast and headed to drama club rehearsal. He was eager to pass off the draft to Mr. Shaw. When he arrived at the drama club room, Mr. Shaw was just opening the door. "You're here early, Mac," he said.

"I couldn't sleep. I was excited about turning in the final draft," Mac replied. He reached into his backpack to pull out the draft. After a few seconds of feeling for it, Mac put down his bag. He pulled out his notebook. He pulled out his play props. He even pulled out his lunch. When there was nothing left in his bag, Mac turned it upside down and started

© 2009 K12 Inc. All rights reserved.

© 2009 K12 Inc. All rights reserved.

Name: _____

/er/ and Prefix *quadr–*

Mystery Words

Choose a word from the box to match each clue below. Write each word next to the clue, on the lines provided in the second column.

worms	Thursday	first	whisper	colors	under
words	winter	purr	fur	girl	bird

Clue	**Word**
1. to talk softly	_____
2. they crawl on the ground	_____
3. season that comes after fall	_____
4. opposite of over	_____
5. before second	_____
6. it keeps animals warm	_____
7. sentences are made of these	_____
8. the noise a cat makes	_____
9. red and blue are two	_____
10. it has wings and a beak	_____
11. a day of the week	_____
12. opposite of boy	_____

© 2009 K12 Inc. All rights reserved.

Name:

Using the Prefix *quadr–*

The prefix *quadr–* means "four." Choose a word from the box to match each definition below. Write each word on the lines provided in the second column.

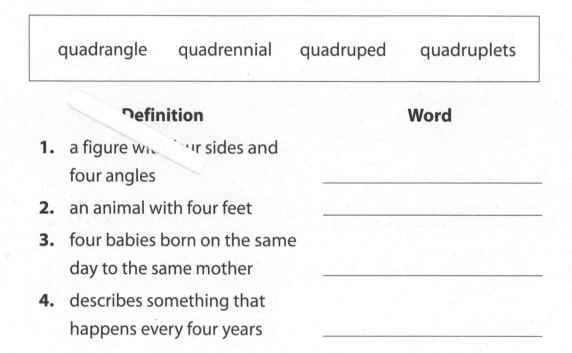

| quadrangle | quadrennial | quadruped | quadruplets |

Definition	Word
1. a figure with four sides and four angles	_____
2. an animal with four feet	_____
3. four babies born on the same day to the same mother	_____
4. describes something that happens every four years	_____

Choose two words from the box above. Write sentences using each word on the lines provided below.

5. _____

_____

6. _____

_____

© 2009 K12 Inc. All rights reserved.

Get Ready

■ Plural possessive nouns show that more than one person, place, thing, or idea has ownership. To form a plural possessive noun, usually you add only an apostrophe to the end of the plural noun. This rule applies to any plural noun that ends in –s.

■ Look at the singular nouns in the first column below, and then look at the plural nouns in the middle column. Notice that to make each noun plural, an –s was simply added to the end of each noun. To make the plural possessive form of the noun, an apostrophe was added to the –s.

Singular Noun	Plural Noun	Plural Possessive Noun
tree	trees	trees' leaves
fly	flies	flies' buzzing

■ But some nouns are irregular, and have plurals that do not end in –s. How do you make an irregular plural noun, such as *oxen* or *teeth*, possessive? To make the possessive of an irregular plural form, you add 's to the plural noun.

■ Look at the singular nouns in the first column below, and then look at the plural nouns in the middle column. Then, notice that 's was added to make each irregular plural possessive noun.

Singular Noun	Irregular Plural Noun	Irregular Plural Possessive Noun
man	men	men's team
mouse	mice	mice's holes

© 2009 K12 Inc. All rights reserved.

Try It

On the lines provided under the proper columns below, fill in the singular possessive form, the plural form, and the plural possessive form of each noun. An example has been done for you.

Noun	Singular Possessive	Plural	Plural Possessive
table	table's	tables	tables'
1. bird	_____	_____	_____
2. goose	_____	_____	_____
man	_____	_____	_____
4. ʾup	_____	_____	_____
5. c ir	_____	_____	_____
6. ox	_____	_____	_____
7. giraffe	_____	_____	_____
8. doll	_____	_____	_____
9. boss	_____	_____	_____
10. beach	_____	_____	_____

© 2009 K12 Inc. All rights reserved.

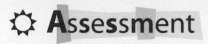
Unit 1 Assessment

Part 1.

Listen to each word as it is read to you. Then write the word on the line provided.

1. _____   4. _____   7. _____

2. _____   5. _____   8. _____

3. _____   6. _____   9. _____

Read each set of three words below. Select the word from each set that contains a long vowel sound and write that word on the line provided below the three words. An example has been done for you.

Example: pan, pail, pant

_____pail_____

10. know, knot, knock   14. use, is, nut   18. weigh, wash, went

_____   _____   _____

11. fast, feed, fowl   15. play, pest, pat   19. music, man, men

_____   _____   _____

12. why, when, who   16. team, tub, tip   20. day, done, drip

_____   _____   _____

13. note, not, knot   17. slip, slid, slide

_____   _____

© 2009 K12 Inc. All rights reserved.

Part 2.

Read the paragraph below. On the lines provided, write five different long double o sound words and five different short double o sound words that are found in the paragraph.

John was cooking dinner for his family. He was going to make noodles with sauce. First, he needed to heat the sauce. He poured it into a pan, and stirred it with a spoon. Next, he took the noodles out of a plastic tube and dropped them into hot water. When they were done, he looked for the wooden bowl. The noodles fit just right in the wooden bowl. Next, he tasted the sauce. It was too hot. He hurt his tongue. But it was done. Finally, John set out the nice, blue plates on the table. This dinner was going to be good!

21. Short Double *o* Sound

_____

_____

_____

_____

_____

22. Long Double *o* Sound

_____

_____

_____

_____

_____

© 2009 K12 Inc. All rights reserved.

Name:

Long Vowels and Prefixes

Part 3.

Read the clues to fill in the words in the crossword.
Hint: Each answer uses a different prefix.

23. **Across**

1. what you put before a base word
2. a vehicle with two wheels
3. a vehicle with one wheel
4. the middle of the week
5. an answer that is not right
6. to make something new again

Down

7. to lose something
8. a train beneath a city
9. to draw a line beneath something
10. an animal with four legs
11. to have an opinion different from someone else's
12. to tell what will happen in the future

© 2009 K12 Inc. All rights reserved.

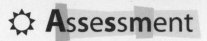

Part 4.

Listen to each word as it is read to you. Write each word in the column for the r-controlled vowel that this word uses.

24. *ar* Words

_____

_____

_____

25. *or* Words

_____

_____

_____

26. *ir* Words

_____

_____

_____

27. *ur* Words

_____

_____

_____

28. *er* Words

_____

_____

_____

29. *ear* Words

_____

_____

_____

© 2009 K12 Inc. All rights reserved.

/k/ and Prefix *kilo*–

Sort the Spellings: /k/

Write each word in the box below in the correct column according to its spelling of the /k/ sound. Then write one new word for each spelling of the /k/ sound. Read all the words aloud.

blackbird	include	checkers	keep	pocket
toothpick	cheek	kid	chicken	cape
brake	coat	cube	cast	kit

c   *k*

_____   _____

_____   _____

_____   _____

_____   _____

New: _____   **New:** _____

ck

_____

_____

_____

_____

New: _____

© 2009 K12 Inc. All rights reserved.

Synonyms and Sentences

The prefix *kilo–* means "one thousand." Choose a word from the box to match each phrase below. Write each word on the line provided next to the matching phrase.

kilogram	kiloliter	kilometer	kilovolt	kilowatt

Phrase   **Word**

1. 1,000 liters   _____

2. about 2.2 pounds   _____

3. 1,000 volts   _____

4. 1,000 watts   _____

5. about 6/10 mile   _____

Choose three words from the box above. On the lines provided below, write sentences using each word that you chose.

6. _____

_____

7. _____

_____

8. _____

_____

74

© 2009 K12 Inc. All rights reserved.

ch and *que* as /k/

In each word, underline all the letters that make the /k/ sound. Then write each word in a sentence.

Hint: One of the words has two spellings of /k/.

1. anchor _____

   _____

2. chemistry _____

   _____

3. antique _____

   _____

4. chrome _____

   _____

5. ache _____

   _____

6. plaque _____

   _____

7. scheme _____

   _____

8. technique _____

   _____

9. unique _____

   _____

10. stomach _____

    _____

© 2009 K12 Inc. All rights reserved.

Prefix Practice

The prefix *tele*– means "over a distance." A *telephone* sends calls over a distance. A *telegram* is a message sent over a distance by code. A *telegraph* is a device for sending telegrams over a distance. On the lines provided, use the hints and what you know about the meaning of *tele*– to write a definition for each word.

1. telescope (noun)

Hint: A scope is a device used for looking at something.

_____

_____

2. television (noun)

Hint: Vision means "the act of seeing."

_____

_____

3. telemarketer (noun)

Hint: A marketer is a person who is selling a product.

_____

_____

4. teleconference (noun)

Hint: A conference is a meeting.

_____

_____

© 2009 K12 Inc. All rights reserved.

A Team Victory

Vicky yanked her bag off its hook. She slammed her locker door shut. She put on her jacket and shoved her hands in her pockets. Then she stormed out of the locker room. Vicky walked home with her head down. She grumbled to herself the whole way. She was upset about the track meet. Vicky could not believe that she hadn't won her race. She had trained every day for months.

© 2009 K12 Inc. All rights reserved.

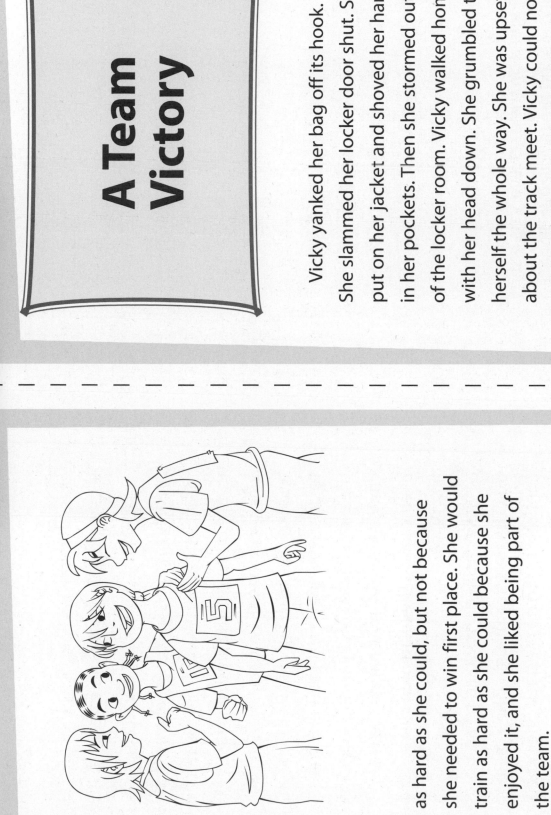

as hard as she could, but not because she needed to win first place. She would train as hard as she could because she enjoyed it, and she liked being part of the team.

© 2009 K12 Inc. All rights reserved.

She jogged on the track every day. She jogged around the block after dinner. She even jogged in the park on the weekends. With all that hard work, Vicky could not believe she lost her race.

© 2009 K12 Inc. All rights reserved.

---

crossed the finish line, Vicky thought her legs were going to crumble beneath her.

Vicky took a moment to catch her breath. Then she asked if the team had made it to the finals. Kay told her that they didn't cross the finish line first. Vicky waited for Kay to finish. Then Kay told her that they finished well enough to go to the finals next month. All of the girls cheered. Vicky was thrilled! She couldn't believe how happy she was, even though the team didn't win first place.

Vicky decided she would never quit the track team again. She would continue to jog on the track. She would still jog in the evenings. She would even jog on the weekends. She would train

© 2009 K12 Inc. All rights reserved.

After the track meet, Vicky decided that she would quit the track team.

She didn't see the point of training so hard if it didn't help her win. She would rather watch television. She thought it would be better to look at the night sky through her telescope after dinner. She would rather talk on the telephone all weekend. Anything would be better than training and not winning, Vicky thought.

The next day, Vicky's friend Kay began talking to her about next week's track meet. Vicky told her that she planned to quit the team. Kay seemed upset. She explained to Vicky that no one wins every race. She didn't know how Vicky could quit something she enjoyed,

© 2009 K12 Inc. All rights reserved.

Then the girls trained until it was time to go home.

On the day of the track meet, Vicky and her teammates were full of excitement. They walked back and forth to try to calm their nerves. They ate healthy snacks to give them energy. They stretched and warmed up. Finally, it was time for their race. The girls took off their track jackets. They walked over to the starting line. They each took their places. Then they waited for the starting gun. The gun sounded and the race began. Each girl ran her leg of the race. Then she passed the baton to the next runner. Vicky was the last member of the team to run. She grabbed the baton from Kay. She ran harder than she had ever run in her life. By the time she

© 2009 K12 Inc. All rights reserved.

just because she lost a race. She also couldn't understand how Vicky could let down her team.

Vicky was shocked by Kay's reaction. She did not think anyone would care if she quit the track team. She did not know how she was letting down the team, either. Kay explained to Vicky that next week's track meet was a key meet. It would determine whether the track team went on to the finals. They needed Vicky to run part of the relay race. Kay told Vicky that the team races were just as important as the individual races. She told Vicky that without her, the team would not have a chance to move on to the finals.

© 2009 K12 Inc. All rights reserved.

Vicky spent the rest of the day thinking. She thought about how she felt when she ran on the track. She thought about what Kay had said. She thought about the rest of the team. Later that day, Vicky went to the track. She knew her teammates would be there. She told them that Kay was right. Vicky now understood that team races were just as important as her own races. She told them she would stay on the team. That meant she would compete in next week's track meet.

Vicky and the rest of the team talked about how next week's meet was a key meet for the team. They planned to train more than usual. They would run every morning and afternoon until the meet.

© 2009 K12 Inc. All rights reserved.

/k/ and Prefix *multi–*

Sort the Spellings: /k/

Write each word in the box below in the correct column according to the spelling of the /k/ sound in the word. Then write one new word of your own for each spelling of the /k/ sound. Read all the words aloud.

Hint: Two of the words each contain two spellings of the /k/ sound, so they belong in two columns.

| arctic | truck | scheme | campus | chrome | keep | locker |
| bucket | cook | unique | desk | plaque | technique | |

c

_____

_____

_____

New: _____

k

_____

_____

_____

New: _____

ck

_____

_____

_____

New: _____

ch

_____

_____

_____

New: _____

que

_____

_____

_____

New: _____

© 2009 K12 Inc. All rights reserved.

Using the Prefix *multi–*

The prefix *multi–* means "many," or "more than two." Choose a word from the box to match each phrase. Write each word in the second column.

multinational	multispeed	
multitalented	multicolored	multilevel

Phrase	**Word**
1. having many colors	_____
2. having more than two speeds	_____
3. consisting of many nations	_____
4. having more than two levels	_____
5. having many talents	_____

Choose three words from the box above. Write a sentence using each word.

6. _____

_____

7. _____

_____

8. _____

_____

© 2009 K12 Inc. All rights reserved.

Get Ready

Commas are used for a variety of reasons. Let's look at some examples of when commas are used to punctuate sentences:

◾ Use a comma to separate words in a series.

A series is a list of items. When you write a list of items in a sentence, separate the items with commas.

> Monday, Tuesday, and Wednesday are my days to feed the cat.

◾ Use a comma in a date between the day of the month and the year.

When you write the month, day, and year of a date, put a comma between the day and the year.

> July 25, 1992

◾ Use a comma between the name of a city and the state or country.

When you write the name of a place, and are using both the name of a city or town and the name of a state or country, put a comma between the name of the city and the name of the state or country.

> Richmond, Virginia　　　　Paris, France

◾ Use a comma with Yes , No, and other words of address.

When you begin a sentence with yes or no, or if you are addressing someone, use a comma.

> Yes, you may go.　　　Hey, let's go.　　　Where should this go, Bob?

◾ Use a comma with quotation marks.

Use a comma after the exact words of the speaker, when the speaker's words come at the beginning of a sentence. Use a comma before the exact words of the speaker, when the speaker's words come at the end of the sentence.

> "Mary, here's your doll," said Mom.　　　Dad said, "Yes, I'd like to go."

© 2009 K12 Inc. All rights reserved.

Try It

Read and answer the following questions. Be sure to use commas.

1. When is your birthday? _____

2. What city and state do you live in?

   _____

3. Would you like to have a snack? (Be sure to answer in a complete

   sentence!) _____

Rewrite the sentences below by adding commas where needed.

4. I packed socks shorts and shirts in my suitcase.

   _____

5. "Can you help me" asked Jen "get this done?"

   _____

6. Hey what's that?

   _____

7. We need apples pears and cherries for the fruit salad.

   _____

8. Chris shouted "Let's go Mike!"

   _____

© 2009 K12 Inc. All rights reserved.

Place the Sound

Read each word in the box aloud. Then write each word in the correct column below. The first one is done for you.

fear	physics	refer	trophy
forget	puff	dolphin	phrase
effort	telephone	alphabet	friendship

/f/ Spelled with *f*

fear
_____

_____

_____

_____

_____

/f/ Spelled with *ph*

_____

_____

_____

_____

_____

Write three sentences. In each sentence, use one word with /f/ spelled with *ph*.

1. _____

_____

2. _____

_____

3. _____

_____

© 2009 K12 Inc. All rights reserved.

Complete the Sentence

The prefix *micro–* means "very small." Read the following words and their definitions. Use the words to complete the sentences below.

Word	Meaning
microwave	a device that heats food using tiny radiation waves
microscope	a device that allows you to see very small things
microsecond	a very short time, much less than a second
microchip	a small electronic piece in a computer
microfilm	film with small pictures of printed text or photographs
microclimate	the climate of a very small area or space

1. Even though it is mostly warm and dry where I live, the woods nearby have their own _____ . The woods are cool and damp.

2. I use a _____ to see things that are too small to see with just my eyes.

3. Sam used the _____ to warm up his lunch.

4. In the library, you can find any story in the newspaper on _____ .

5. I took one _____ out and the whole computer stopped working.

6. The flash of lightning lasted only for a _____ .

© 2009 K12 Inc. All rights reserved.

Alphabet Soup Adventures

"Another boring Saturday," Phil grumbled to his father. "Every Saturday it's the same thing: oatmeal for breakfast, clean the house, soup for lunch, work in the yard, and meat loaf for dinner. I wish things were more exciting around here. Sometimes I wonder how it would be to live someone else's life."

"I'm sorry you think things are so boring," Phil's father said. "Try to enjoy

© 2009 K12 Inc. All rights reserved.

dishes snapped Phil from his daydream. He looked around the kitchen and was glad to be home. He took a small taste of his soup. It was finally cool enough to eat. Phil spooned his alphabet soup into his mouth. This time, he didn't look down at the letters.

"Thanks for the soup, Dad," Phil said between spoonfuls.

"You're welcome. It's not too boring to eat?" Dad asked with a smile.

"No way! I've decided I like our Saturdays just the way they are. Who needs to be famous or have feasts? Those things just lead to craziness and aching stomachs. There's nothing like alphabet soup and Saturdays with my dad!" Phil said. Then he finished his soup and helped his dad clean up.

© 2009 K12 Inc. All rights reserved.

your boring alphabet soup while I clean the kitchen."

Phil blew on his soup to cool it down. He looked at the letters floating in the bowl. He saw several letters that had formed a word. "F-a-m-e, fame," he said.

As he stared at the word, Phil began to daydream. He imagined himself wearing

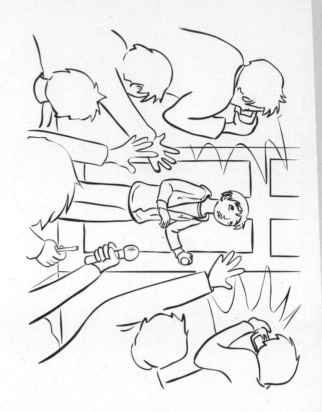

© 2009 K12 Inc. All rights reserved.

I could always start with the frozen yogurt, fudge, or French toast!" Phil stuck his fork in the dish closest to him and began eating. He filled his mouth with something from every bowl, plate, and cup on the table. He loved the flavor of each food he tasted. He walked to the middle of the table and continued eating. As he moved to the end of the table, he slowed down.

"I don't think I can take one more bite," Phil said, as he dropped his fork. He sat completely still for a moment. Then he leaned over and put his head on the table. Phil felt sick. His stomach hurt worse than it had ever hurt before. "All this food doesn't seem so great now," he groaned as he held his stomach. Just then, the sound of Dad putting away

© 2009 K12 Inc. All rights reserved.

dark sunglasses and driving a fancy car. He drove the car through a neighborhood of fancy houses and parked in front of the biggest one. He walked into the house and looked around. He saw someone dusting in the living room. He saw a person cleaning the swimming pool in the backyard. He saw someone else doing yard work. As Phil looked around his big house with people doing all the hard work for him, a man walked up to him.

"Would you like an afternoon snack, sir? I can have the chef prepare whatever you like," the man said.

"Wow, that sounds great, but I'm not hungry. I think I'll drive to the beach. I'll be back for dinner," Phil answered.

"Very well. What would you like for dinner, sir?" the man asked.

© 2009 K12 Inc. All rights reserved.

As soon as he said the word, Phil was in another daydream. This time, he sat at the end of a long table. It was full of all of his favorite foods. "This looks fabulous!" Phil shouted. He picked up his fork and looked over the feast. "I don't know what to eat first, the french fries, fried chicken, or fish sticks! Of course,

© 2009 K12 Inc. All rights reserved.

"I'd love a pizza with lots of cheese and no vegetables. Oh, and I'd like ice cream for dessert!" Phil said. He was thrilled to pick anything he wanted to eat. He was even happier that he didn't have to eat meat loaf for dinner again.

Phil turned to leave. He took a step outside and was greeted with flashing lights. He realized the bright lights were cameras flashing. People were trying to take his photograph. They began shouting out questions and crowding around him. They pushed toward him to get his autograph. Phil ran to his car. He jumped inside, locked the doors, and drove away. *Whew, I'm glad I got away from them. That was a little too much attention,* Phil thought. Then he saw a group of cars following him. He looked

© 2009 K12 Inc. All rights reserved.

at the cars driving next to him. They had cameras pointed at him. The cameras started flashing again.

Phil began to worry. He was having trouble driving with so many cars around him. He could barely see the road with all of the flashing in his eyes. *I wish all of these people would just go away! I've had enough!* Phil thought. At that moment, Dad put some dishes in the sink. The noise startled Phil from his daydream. He looked around the kitchen and realized he was home.

Phil looked down at his bowl. Steam was still drifting from the soup. He blew on it again to cool it down. Phil looked at the letters floating in the soup. He saw another word. "F-e-a-s-t, feast," he said.

© 2009 K12 Inc. All rights reserved.

Crossword Puzzle

Read the clues to fill in the words in the crossword.
Hint: Each answer uses the letters *ph* to make the /f/ sound.

Across

1. something not real, or fake

2. all the letters we use to spell words

3. a temporary stage

Down

4. a diagram that uses dots, lines, or bars to compare things or show how things change

5. a hurricane

3. an unreasonable fear of something

6. the son of a person's sister or brother

© 2009 K12 Inc. All rights reserved.

Name that Word!

The prefix *out–* means "outside of" or "to go beyond." Add the prefix *out–* to the words in the box to make new words that fit the clues below.

number	play	do
weigh	last	run

1. Write the word that means "to run faster than."

   _____

2. Write the word that means "to be greater in weight than."

   _____

3. Write the word that means "to play better than."

   _____

4. Write the word that means "to do better than."

   _____

5. Write the word that means "to last longer than."

   _____

6. Write the word that means "to be more in number than."

   _____

© 2009 K12 Inc. All rights reserved.

Get Ready

▚ Adjectives describe nouns. A proper adjective describes a proper noun. The most common proper adjectives are those formed from place names. Study this list of examples.

Proper Noun	Proper Adjective
America	American
Norway	Norwegian
France	French
Texas	Texan
East	Eastern

▚ At other times, a proper adjective is formed from a person's name.

Proper Noun	Proper Adjective
Dylan	Dylanesque
Freud	Freudian
Calvin	Calvinistic

▚ Sometimes, proper adjectives can even be brand names.

Kodak® camera

Xerox® copier

Kleenex® tissues

▚ Finally, proper adjectives include professional or family titles.

Dr. Winger

Mrs. Stone

Pastor John

© 2009 K12 Inc. All rights reserved.

Try It

Read each sentence. Underline the proper adjective, or adjectives, in each sentence.

1. The African drums were on display at the museum.

2. The poem that she wrote was Shakespearean in style.

3. My favorite cake is German chocolate cake.

4. Mr. Santos is Cuban; he was born in Cuba.

5. In Virginia, Route 29 is known as Lee Highway, while in South Carolina, it is known as Wade Hampton Boulevard.

6. We went to the Japanese steak house for my birthday.

7. Next year, we are going to see a Broadway play.

8. Dad will make Belgian waffles on Saturday.

9. We are moving to the Pacific Northwest this summer.

10. I think that Dr. Fishtone went to Eastern Europe over the holiday.

© 2009 K12 Inc. All rights reserved.

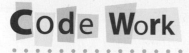

Find the Word

Look up each word in a dictionary. Write the definition of each word, in your own words, on the lines provided below.

1. guilty
Definition: _____

_____

2. guard
Definition: _____

_____

3. guitar
Definition: _____

_____

4. guess
Definition: _____

_____

5. guide
Definition: _____

_____

Choose two of the words above, and write each word in a sentence.

6. Word: _____

Sentence: _____

_____

7. Word: _____

Sentence: _____

_____

© 2009 K12 Inc. All rights reserved.

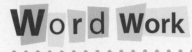

Mystery Words

Choose a word from the box to match each clue below. Write each word on the line provided in the second column.

overreact	overcook	oversleep	overdress	overspend
overeat	overload	overinflate	overheat	

Clue   **Word**

1. to wear clothes that are
     too fancy for an occasion   _____

2. to get much too hot   _____

3. to put too big of a load on   _____

4. to sleep too much or too late _____

5. to inflate too much   _____

6. to cook for too long   _____

7. to have too much of a reaction _____

8. to eat too much   _____

9. to spend too much money   _____

© 2009 K12 Inc. All rights reserved.

Gail's Hard Lesson

When Gail was five years old, she painted a mug for her mother. She made sure to include all her favorite things on the mug: a hairy bug, a spotted dog, a green frog, a gray goat, and a pink pig. Gail put the mug in a brown bag. Gail had a big smile on her face when she handed the bag to her mother. Her mother pulled out the gift and turned

© 2009 K12 Inc. All rights reserved.

---

favorite colors and things on one side, and on the other side, I'll paint your favorite colors and things. I know it won't replace the one I broke, but I hope you'll love it just as much," Gail said. She walked over to her mother and gave her a big hug. Her mother knew the hug said, "I'm sorry," and "Thank you," so Mom squeezed back to let Gail know that everything was all right.

© 2009 K12 Inc. All rights reserved.

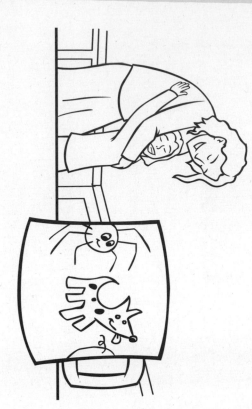

to Gail. Her mother's smile matched her own. "Thank you, Gail. This is the best gift anyone has ever given me. It's lovely. I'll use this mug every day," she said.
Then she scooped Gail into a big hug...

© 2009 K12 Inc. All rights reserved.

© 2009 K12 Inc. All rights reserved.

"Ground me for life?" Gail asked. She knew her mother was very upset, and Gail expected to be in big trouble for a long time.

"I can tell that you feel very bad for what you've done. I hope you've learned your lesson," her mother said.

"I have learned my lesson. I'll never throw my ball in the house again, and I'll always listen to what you say," Gail stated.

"I'm glad to hear that. Since it was an accident and you've learned your lesson, I don't think I need to ground you. However, there is something I want you to do. I want you to make me another mug," her mother said.

"Of course I'll make you another mug, Mom! I'll start right now. I'll paint my...

As the years passed, the mug became chipped and cracked. Gail's mother didn't mind. She still used it every day. Sometimes she used the mug for coffee. Sometimes she used it for tea. Some days the mug held milk. Other days it held water. Gail's mother loved her mug, cracks and all.

One day, Gail was throwing her ball in the kitchen. Her mother sat at the table drinking milk from her favorite mug.

"Gail, I've told you many times not to throw your ball in the house. Please take it outside before you break something," her mother said sternly.

Gail took her ball outside. She threw the ball in the air and caught it on

© 2009 K12 Inc. All rights reserved.

"Well, Gail, I'm very sad that you broke the mug. I'm also upset that you did something I asked you not to do. I can think of only one thing to do," her mother responded.

© 2009 K12 Inc. All rights reserved.

the way down. Gail was very good at playing ball. She caught it every time. As Gail played outside, the sun began to set. When she could no longer see her ball, Gail went back inside the house.

The next day, Gail looked out the window and saw that it was raining. She was upset that she couldn't go outside to play. She came up with things to do inside until it stopped raining. First, she drew pictures. Then she colored the pictures. Next, she played board games. She even spent time chewing bubble gum and trying to blow the biggest bubble ever. Finally, Gail became bored. She grabbed her ball and began tossing it in the air. Gail walked around the

house, tossing and catching the ball. She walked down the hall. She walked through the living room. She walked around the dining room. When Gail walked into the kitchen, she was very focused on her ball. She was not paying attention to where she was walking.

Gail took a few steps, and then she tripped on the kitchen rug. Gail watched in horror as the ball hit her leg and knocked over her mother's favorite mug. Before Gail or her mother could catch it, the mug fell to the floor. It shattered into tiny pieces. "Oh, Mom, I'm so sorry!" Gail said. She felt terrible, and her mother could tell. "I should have never been throwing my ball in the house. Now I've broken your favorite mug. I feel awful," Gail cried.

Sort the Spellings: /j/

Read each word in the box aloud. Write each word in the correct column according to the spelling of the /j/ sound. The first one is done for you.

giant	trudge	gym	refrigerate
gem	badge	agent	judge
fudge	edge	bridge	suggest

g   **dge**

giant
_____   _____

_____   _____

_____   _____

_____   _____

_____   _____

Write three sentences. In each sentence, use one word with /j/ spelled *dge*.

1. _____
   _____

2. _____
   _____

3. _____
   _____

© 2009 K12 Inc. All rights reserved.

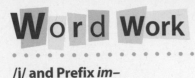

Name:

Complete the Sentence

The prefix *im–* means "not." Read the list of *im–* words and their meanings. Then use the words to complete the sentences below.

Word	Meaning
impossible	not possible
improper	not proper or not appropriate
immobile	not mobile or not moving
imperfect	flawed, or not perfect
impatient	not patient
immature	acting younger than one's age

1. My mom still likes to color, even though it is an _____ thing to do as an adult.

2. It is _____ to throw food in a restaurant.

3. The _____ statue has a bumpy nose and arms that are too long.

4. John was too _____ to wait any longer for Jeremy, so he left.

5. It is _____ for pigs to fly.

6. The scared rabbit stayed _____, hoping that the hawk wouldn't see him.

© 2009 K12 Inc. All rights reserved.

Gene's Challenge

"Ha! Ha! Look at Gene. He can't even jump rope without getting all tangled up!" Jade laughed. She was pointing at Gene and talking loud enough for everyone in the gym to hear. All the other kids were staring at him. Gene was embarrassed. He wanted to crawl under a giant rock and hide. "Hey, everyone, look at me. Watch what I can do," Jade shouted. Then she grabbed her jump rope and began skipping around the

© 2009 K12 Inc. All rights reserved.

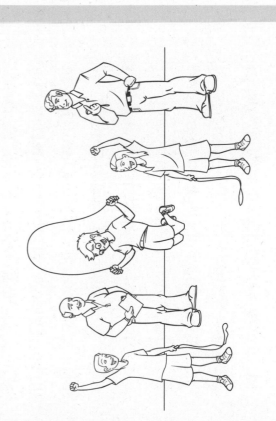

"Congratulations, Gene. You beat the rest of us by a mile!" Jade said. Gene smiled as one of the judges handed Gene his ribbon. He couldn't believe how far he had come in three weeks. He also couldn't imagine how much better he would be for next year's challenge!

© 2009 K12 Inc. All rights reserved.

gym. First, she jumped on one foot. Next, she crossed the rope while she jumped. Jade was great at jumping rope, and she knew it.

© 2009 K12 Inc. All rights reserved.

Gene threw the rope over his head and started jumping. He wobbled a little at first, but he quickly found his groove. He jumped calmly. He controlled his breathing, just as he had practiced. He tuned out all of the distractions.

Gene jumped and jumped without looking at anyone else. That's why he didn't notice when everyone else in his challenge group had finished jumping. He continued jumping until the rope caught on his heel and he had to stop. That's when Gene saw the others in his challenge staring at him. This time, they weren't making fun of him. This time, they were cheering for him because he had won the challenge!

© 2009 K12 Inc. All rights reserved.

Gene was glad everyone was watching Jade. Now he could sneak into the locker room. He really wanted to get away from the jeers and snickering. On his way to the locker room, Gene saw a flyer posted on the door. It was for the neighborhood jump-rope challenge. *I really want to get better at jumping rope,* he thought. *The jump-rope challenge is three weeks away. If I practice really hard, maybe I'll be good enough to enter.*

For the next three weeks, Gene worked hard. He jumped rope every day. He also jumped on the weekends. He asked his brother for help. He researched tips to improve his skills. He talked about the challenge with his parents and friends. By the time the day of the challenge arrived, Gene was

© 2009 K12 Inc. All rights reserved.

like to thank you for supporting the neighborhood jump-rope challenge," one of the judges said. "We're going to have several challenges going at one time, so please make sure you listen when we tell you where to go."

Gene listened for his name and walked over to the others in his challenge group. He became nervous when Jade walked over and stood beside him. *What if I mess up and she laughs at me?* he wondered. *No, I can't think like that. I've worked really hard. As long as I do my best, I'll be happy with myself,* he thought. "Good luck, Jade," Gene offered with a smile. Just then, the whistle blew.

© 2009 K12 Inc. All rights reserved.

much better than he had been that day in the gym. He knew he could enter the challenge and be proud. "Today's the day," Gene said to his family.

"Good luck, Gene! Just try your hardest and have fun," his mom encouraged him.

"Remember everything we've worked on these past few weeks," his brother reminded him.

"We're all proud of you, Gene. We'll see you there," his father said.

Gene put on his jacket, grabbed his bag, and ran all the way to the community center. He sped through the crowd. Then he darted into the locker room. After changing his clothes, Gene walked over to the registration table. He looked at the list of challenges.

© 2009 K12 Inc. All rights reserved.

Some challenges focused on speed. Some focused on tricks. Gene wrote his name down for the time challenge. This challenge tested how long a person could jump rope without stopping.

Gene knew he was better at jumping rope than he had been three weeks ago. He also knew he could jump rope for a long time now. What he didn't know was whether he could jump rope long enough to win the challenge.

Gene walked over to the warm-up area. He looked around the gym. He saw kids and parents sitting in the stands. He waved when he found his family. Gene also saw judges sitting at a table. They were wearing badges and holding stopwatches. Gene's stomach started to tickle. "Good afternoon, everyone. We'd

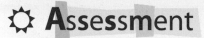
Unit 2 Assessment

Part 1.

Write each word in the box in the correct column below, according to the spelling of the /f/ or /k/ sound. The first one in each column has been done for you.

phantom	pick	dolphin	headache	atmosphere	king
face	chafe	chorus	effort	check	pack
school	act	orphan	kindling	kept	crop
protect	crime	fetch	charisma	graph	pocket
ferry	think	stomach	tickle	direct	prank

1. /f/ Spelled _ph_

phantom

_____

_____

_____

_____

2. /f/ Spelled _f_

ferry

_____

_____

_____

_____

3. /k/ Spelled _c_

crime

_____

_____

_____

_____

4. /k/ Spelled _ch_

headache

_____

_____

_____

5. /k/ Spelled _ck_

check

_____

_____

_____

6. /k/ Spelled _k_

king

_____

_____

_____

© 2009 K12 Inc. All rights reserved.

Part 2.

Read the paragraphs below. In the columns provided, write the following words found in the paragraphs: five words with /g/ spelled *gu*; five with /g/ spelled *gg* or *gh*; five with /j/ spelled *j*; and five with /j/ spelled *dge*.
Hint: Two words belong in more than one column.

Susan was taking guitar lessons. Susan had never had lessons before. She had played around with the instrument, but she was just guessing. She really couldn't judge what she was doing. Most of what she had played sounded ghastly. When she had tried to play, it sounded like an aggravated ghost had taken over the instrument. The noises put her on edge.

But now she was learning for real. Her teacher guided her. He was kind of a fussbudget, but he was nice. She had pledged to her teacher that she would practice. She practiced a lot, giggling and jumping up and down whenever she got a piece to sound right. If she ever forgot to practice, she felt guilty. Her favorite song was called "The Juggling Guest." It was a happy, jaunty tune.

Susan was learning fast. She used to be bad at this. Now she felt like a full-fledged musician.

7.   /g/ Spelled *gu*

_____

_____

_____

_____

8.   /g/ Spelled *gg* or *gh*

_____

_____

_____

_____

© 2009 K12 Inc. All rights reserved.

9. /j/ Spelled *j*	10. /j/ Spelled *dge*
_____	_____
_____	_____
_____	_____
_____	_____
_____	_____

Part 3.

Choose a prefix from the box to match each definition below. Write each prefix on the line provided.

kilo–	tele–	multi–	out–
micro–	over–	im–	

11. several or many _____

12. very small _____

13. in a manner that goes beyond _____

14. too much or too many _____

15. not _____

16. over a distance _____

17. thousand _____

© 2009 K12 Inc. All rights reserved.

Part 4.

Read each definition. Then choose the correct prefix to complete the word that matches each definition. Write that word on the line provided.

18. Definition: not allowed by the law

Word: _____ legal *(multi–, il–, over–)*

19. Definition: to become way too hot

Word: _____ heat *(re–, in–, over–)*

20. Definition: not smooth

Word: _____ regular *(micro–, kilo–, ir–)*

21. Definition: tool used to see very small things

Word: _____ scope *(micro–, im–, out–)*

22. Definition: having many colors

Word: _____ colored *(un–, tele–, multi–)*

23. Definition: item used to talk over a distance

Word: _____ phone *(out–, kilo–, tele–)*

24. Definition: not correct or not right

Word: _____ proper *(im–, micro–, out–)*

© 2009 K12 Inc. All rights reserved.

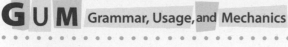
Get Ready

- *A*, *an*, and *the* are articles. Articles describe nouns. This means that articles are a type of adjective.

- There are two kinds of articles—definite articles and indefinite articles.
  Definite article: describes a specific or defined noun

  The is a definite article.

  Indefinite article: describes a general or unspecified noun

  A and *an* are indefinite articles.

- When do you use *a*, and when do you use *an*? Use *a* before a word that starts with a consonant sound. Use *an* before a word that starts with a vowel sound.

  Definite Article: the car
  The car refers to specific or known car.

  Indefinite Article: a car
  A car refers to any car.

  Definite Article: the umbrella
  The umbrella refers to a specific or known umbrella.

  Indefinite Article: an umbrella
  An umbrella refers to any umbrella.

© 2009 K12 Inc. All rights reserved.

Try It

Read the sentences. Then underline the articles in each sentence.

1. The brown dog played with a squeaky toy.

2. I have an uncle who lives in the state of Maine.

3. Put the tin cans in a bin for recycling, not in the trash.

4. Tom had the last piece of cake at the party.

5. A cat ran across the path.

6. Bob has the flu.

© 2009 K12 Inc. All rights reserved.

/s/ and Suffix –ation

/s/ Spelled *sc*

Choose a word from the box to match each definition below. Write each word on the line provided in the second column. Then underline the letter or letters in each word that make the /s/ sound.

descend scent scissors adolescent scene crescent ascend

Definition	**Word**
1. to lower or come down	_____
2. a view or picture	_____
3. a phase of the moon	_____
4. a teenager	_____
5. an instrument used for cutting	_____
6. the opposite of *descend*	_____
7. a smell	_____

Choose three of the words above and write each word in a sentence.

8. _____

_____

9. _____

_____

10. _____

_____

© 2009 K12 Inc. All rights reserved.

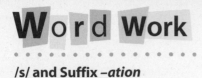

The Suffix –*ation*

Add the suffix –*ation* to each of the following verbs and write the new words on the lines. An example has been done for you.

Example: educate + ation = ___education___

1. locate + ation = _____

2. alter + ation = _____

3. inspire + ation = _____

4. starve + ation = _____

5. expect + ation = _____

6. install + ation = _____

7. motivate + ation = _____

8. consider + ation = _____

9. declare + ation = _____

10. dehydrate + ation = _____

Choose two of the words that you created above, and write each word in a sentence on the lines provided below.

11. _____

_____

12. _____

_____

© 2009 K12 Inc. All rights reserved.

Sand Sculpture Scenes

"The car is loaded. I packed sunscreen, chairs, and the umbrella. I also packed an ice chest and snacks. I think we're ready to go," Grace said to her uncle.

"Did you remember your camera?" her uncle asked.

"It's right here around my neck. It was the first thing I grabbed this morning!" Grace responded. She didn't want to leave the sand sculpture

© 2009 K12 Inc. All rights reserved.

"Why do you say that?" Grace asked.

"Well, that bag of groceries is making me hungry!" her uncle answered.

"I agree! Let's go eat our snacks and take a break. We have plenty of time to see the rest. Besides, my finger is getting tired from taking so many pictures!" Grace and her uncle laughed as they walked to their spot. They ate their snacks and then walked around the rest of the competition. Grace took pictures and talked to her uncle about each entry.

When it was time to leave, Grace reached down to pick up a seashell. "I think I'll take this as a keepsake," she said to her uncle.

"I think that's a great idea," he responded. Then he reached down to pick up a seashell of his own.

© 2009 K12 Inc. All rights reserved.

© 2009 K12 Inc. All rights reserved.

the competition was the creativity of

prove it. The thing she liked most about

a little girl, and she had the photos to

competition every year since she was

competition. Grace had been to the

of every entry. Grace had been to the

competition without at least one photo

© 2009 K12 Inc. All rights reserved.

Grace and her uncle moved on to a kitchen scene. The builders had sculpted a kitchen sink full of sand dishes. The faucet was running sand water, and sand soapsuds topped some of the dishes. Beside the sink, the builders included a sand bag of sand groceries. They even sculpted celery, rice, and cereal sticking out from the top! Grace was almost speechless as she looked at the scene. She couldn't believe the details the builders had included. "This is definitely my favorite entry," she stated. "I hope it wins first place."

"It is pretty impressive," her uncle agreed. "It might be just a little too realistic, though," he added.

the builders. They didn't just build sand castles. They built people, animals, food, and more, all out of sand! Grace was always amazed by each entry.

Once on the road, Grace talked nonstop about the sand sculpture competition. She talked about her favorite entries from years past. She also talked about what she'd like to see this year. Grace had only one thing on her mind, and that was the sand sculpture competition.

After driving for a while, Grace's uncle slowed to a stop. "We're here," he said. He parked the car and Grace jumped out.

"This is a great parking spot! Leaving earlier this year really made a difference," she noted.

© 2009 K12 Inc. All rights reserved.

Grace's uncle pointed out. They saw a sand garage full of sand tools. A sand hammer, a sand screwdriver, and a sand saw sat on top of the sand workbench. Grace took extra pictures of this entry. She thought her uncle might like one of those for himself. From the garage entry,

© 2009 K12 Inc. All rights reserved.

Grace and her uncle unloaded the car. Then they headed toward the beach. "This is the perfect spot. Let's set up our stuff here. There aren't tons of people on this end. Plus, we're not too far from the entries. We'll probably face fewer crowds if we start at the end and make our way from there," Grace said.

"Sounds like a plan. Let's get going," her uncle responded.

The first entry that they saw was a sailboat made of sand. It was surrounded by sand seals swimming in a sea of sand. Grace snapped her first photo. Then they walked over to a sand surfer. He was balanced on his sand surfboard, propped up on a sand wave. Grace snapped her second picture. The third entry Grace and her uncle saw was

an undersea scene. It had fish, plants, and a giant octopus, all made of sand! Grace snapped away. "I think that was the last entry focused on ocean life and activities. I wonder what's next," Grace said to her uncle.

They walked over to the next entry. It was a sand band. A sand drummer and saxophone player were putting on a concert. The sculptors even sculpted people dancing in the crowd. Grace giggled as she snapped her photo. Next, they walked over to a sand deck of playing cards. The ace, king, and queen were the only cards showing from the deck. Grace pointed her camera and snapped another photo.

"It looks like we're about to see the entries showing scenes from homes,"

© 2009 K12 Inc. All rights reserved.

© 2009 K12 Inc. All rights reserved.

Word Match

Match the correct words from the box with the definitions listed below. Write the word on the line provided next to each definition. In each word, underline the letter or letters that make the /sh/ sound. Then read the words aloud.

> machine   mustache   chef
>
> parachute   brochure

1. the hair on a man's upper lip _____

2. a device that opens like an umbrella to slow the fall of a person or thing dropping from a plane _____

3. a cook _____

4. a device that performs a task _____

5. a booklet _____

Choose three words from the box above. On the lines provided below, write sentences that use each of the three words.

6. _____

_____

7. _____

_____

8. _____

_____

© 2009 K12 Inc. All rights reserved.

Who's Who

The suffix –*or* means "one who does something." For example, a supervisor is "one who supervises." Match the words containing the suffix –*or* to their descriptions below. Write each word on the line provided.

decorator	editor	demonstrator	counselor
actor	governor	director	inventor

1. one who acts _____

2. one who demonstrates _____
(shows) by actions

3. one who edits _____

4. one who decorates and _____
furnishes rooms

5. one who governs _____

6. one who directs _____

7. one who gives advice _____

8. one who invents _____

Choose two words from the box above. On the lines provided below, write a sentence that uses each word.

9. _____

_____

10. _____

_____

© 2009 K12 Inc. All rights reserved.

New Music Changes Old Ideas

"Here's your new sheet music. You have one week to practice. Next Monday, we'll have tryouts for first chair," Bruce's band teacher said as he passed out the music at the end of practice. Bruce glanced at the new music and put it in his folder. He was not worried. He was a gifted saxophone player and he was able to learn music quickly. He had been first chair all year. No one had been able to play their sax better than Bruce.

© 2009 K12 Inc. All rights reserved.

"We'll work together and both improve in no time!" Bruce said. From that day forward, Bruce practiced his sax every day. He knew his natural gift could only take him so far. To be really great, he needed to practice.

© 2009 K12 Inc. All rights reserved.

© 2009 K12 Inc. All rights reserved.

"I better start practicing tonight. It usually takes me a few days to learn new music. I want to make sure I can play this song well. I really want to win first chair this time," Bruce heard Trish tell

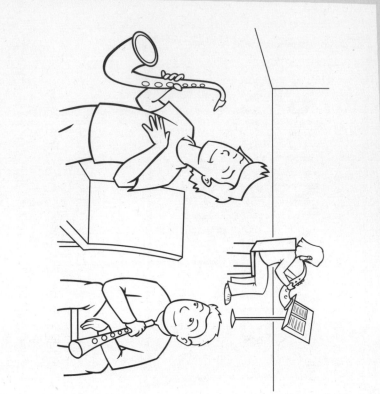

© 2009 K12 Inc. All rights reserved.

took a deep breath and began playing. Her notes were on key and at the right tempo. Her fingers seemed to know the song without any help from her eyes. Bruce could tell that her practice had paid off. Trish's tryout was flawless. When she removed her sax from her lips, a huge smile was revealed. Trish was proud of her performance, and Bruce could understand why. He was disappointed when their band teacher appointed Trish first chair, but he wasn't surprised. Bruce turned to Trish. "Nice job, Trish. You deserved to win first chair. Maybe you can help me practice the piece," he said.

"Thanks, Bruce. I'll certainly help you," Trish replied. "I'd really like it if you helped me, too. My sight-reading skills could use some work."

her friend. Trish also played the sax. She was good, but not as good as Bruce. She was usually second or third chair. Bruce was certain he would beat her this time around, too.

For the next week, Bruce noticed Trish practicing each day. Before band practice, he saw her working on the new music while he hung out with his friends. She looked very focused. He also noticed that she stayed behind after band practice as he headed home. She did not seem to mind putting in extra time working on the new music. Bruce decided he would practice a little over the weekend. He was convinced he would not need to practice as much as Trish had.

© 2009 K12 Inc. All rights reserved.

The air filled his sax and the notes came out smoothly. Bruce tapped his foot to keep tempo. After several flawless measures, Bruce played a wrong note. Several notes later, his sax let out a slight squeak. Bruce remained calm. He knew he could make a few mistakes and still win first chair. He was near the end of the song when he accidentally slurred two notes together. Then he held a note too long. When he finished, Bruce was quite relieved. This song had been a little more challenging than those in the past. However, even with his few mistakes, he was confident he would remain first chair.

Trish was next. Bruce couldn't help but notice how calm Trish looked, bringing her sax up to her mouth. She

© 2009 K12 Inc. All rights reserved.

Bruce had a busy weekend. He played games with his sister and played at the park with his friends. He rode his bike around the block and fixed his skateboard. He watched movies and read. He walked his dog and cleaned his room. What Bruce did not do over the weekend was practice his sheet music.

On Monday morning, Bruce got ready for band practice. That's when he realized that he had forgotten to practice the new sheet music over the weekend. He was still not worried. *I'm pretty good at sight-reading music,* he thought to himself. *I'm sure I'll do fine.*

When Bruce walked into the band room, Trish was already seated with her sax in hand. She seemed to be playing the song with no problem. *Must*

© 2009 K12 Inc. All rights reserved.

© 2009 K12 Inc. All rights reserved.

be pretty easy if she's playing it so well, Bruce thought. *This will be a piece of cake.* Bruce set down his sax case and opened it. He assembled his instrument and began warming up. Before he had a chance to look over his sheet music, his band teacher walked in the room.

"I hope you've all practiced the sheet music I passed out last week. We're going to begin today's session with first-chair tryouts. Last time, we started with the flutes. Today, I'd like to start with the saxophone section," his band teacher announced. Bruce pulled out his sheet music and prepared to go first. He knew this was when his sight-reading skills would come in handy. He took a quick look at the notes on the page. Then he took a deep breath and started to play.

Name: _____

What Am I?

Draw a line from each word in the first column to its meaning in the second column.

Word	**Meaning**
1. social	important
2. official	different from others
3. special	friendly
4. artificial	unnatural
5. beneficial	helpful
6. crucial	a person in authority

Choose four words from above. On the lines provided below, write a sentence for each word.

7. _____

_____

8. _____

_____

9. _____

_____

10. _____

_____

© 2009 K12 Inc. All rights reserved.

Name:

The Suffix *–ous*

The suffix *–ous* means "full of or having." When adding *–ous* to a base word that ends in *e*, drop the *e* before adding the suffix. When adding *–ous* to a base word that ends in *y*, change the *y* to an *i* before adding the suffix.

Read each word in the first column. In the second column, write each word with the suffix *–ous* added to it. In the third column, write the new word's meaning. The first one has been done for you.

Word	Word + Suffix *–ous*	Meaning
1. hazard	hazardous	having dangers and risks
2. glory		
3. vary		
4. joy		
5. danger		
6. fame		
7. nerve		
8. mountain		

© 2009 K12 Inc. All rights reserved.

Get Ready

▣ An adjective describes a person, a place, or a thing. Three types of adjectives are positive adjectives, comparative adjectives, and superlative adjectives.

▣ Positive adjectives describe one or more persons, places, or things.

> Bill is *tall*.
>
> Sam and Matt are *smart*.
>
> This is *fun*.

▣ Comparative adjectives compare two persons, places, or things, or two groups of persons, places, or things. Comparative adjectives are usually formed by adding *–er* to the positive adjective. Sometimes, you put the word more before the adjective.

> Bill is *taller* than Joe.
>
> Sam and Matt are *smarter* than Tom.
>
> Football is *more fun* than soccer.

▣ Superlative adjectives compare three or more persons, places, or things. Superlative adjectives are usually formed by adding *–est* to the positive adjective. Sometimes, you put the word most before the adjective.

> Of the five of us, Bill is the *tallest* person in the family.
>
> Of all the people I know, Sam and Matt are the *smartest*.
>
> Of all the sports I play, basketball is the *most fun*.

© 2009 K12 Inc. All rights reserved.

Try It

On the line provided next to each phrase, write "P" if the adjective is positive, write "C" if the adjective is comparative, or write "S" if the adjective is superlative.

1. smarter student _____
2. loudest yell _____
3. fast runner _____
4. prettier picture _____
5. smarter student _____

6. highest building _____
7. funniest joke _____
8. tiny baby _____
9. most understanding _____
10. hard hit _____

11. On the lines provided below, write a sentence using a positive adjective.

_____

_____

12. On the lines provided below, write a sentence using a comparative adjective.

_____

_____

13. On the lines provided below, write a sentence using a superlative adjective.

_____

_____

© 2009 K12 Inc. All rights reserved.

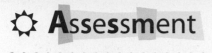
Unit 3 Assessment

Part 1.

Write each word in the box in the correct column below according to the spelling of the /s/ and /sh/ sounds. The first one in each column is done for you.

brochure	yes	safe	twice	face
blush	Michigan	bus	dish	machine
city	shade	scenic	this	crescent
descend	concert	clash	chef	plus
scent	scene	recycle	fresh	Chicago

1. /s/ Spelled s

bus
_____
_____
_____
_____

2. /s/ Spelled c

city
_____
_____
_____
_____

3. /s/ Spelled sc

crescent
_____
_____
_____
_____

4. /sh/ Spelled sh

blush
_____
_____
_____
_____

5. /sh/ Spelled ch

brochure
_____
_____
_____
_____

© 2009 K12 Inc. All rights reserved.

Part 2.

In each sentence, underline the words that contain the /s/ or /sh/ sound.

6. Ascend and descend are opposites.

7. We enjoyed the scenery during the short train ride to Chicago.

8. The candy bar costs 55 cents.

9. I had to sharpen my pencil before I could begin working.

10. Bruce asked Alice for advice about moving to Michigan.

Part 3.

Listen to each word that is read to you. Write each word on the line provided.

11. _____   16. _____

12. _____   17. _____

13. _____   18. _____

14. _____   19. _____

15. _____   20. _____

© 2009 K12 Inc. All rights reserved.

Part 4.

Read each definition and base word. Circle the suffix that must be added to the base word to make it match the definition. Then, on the line provided, write the base word with the correct suffix added to it. The first one has been done for you.

Definition	Base Word	Base Word with Suffix Added
the state of being inspired or encouraged	inspire	(–ation –ist, –ous) inspiration
21. a reporter who gathers, prepares, and sends out news	journal	(–ation, –ist, –ous) _____
22. the art or skill of leading people	leader	(–ist –ous, –ship) _____
23. one who shows how to do something	demonstrate	(–ation, –or, –ous) _____
24. one who gives advice	counsel	(–or, –ous, –ship) _____
25. anxious or full of anxiety	nerve	(–ation, –ist, –ous) _____
26. having several different kinds	vary	(–ist, –or, –ous) _____

© 2009 K12 Inc. All rights reserved.

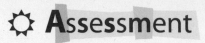
Part 5.

Read each base word and its definition. Then add to each base word the suffix that would make the word match the definition. Write the new word on the line provided below. An example has been done for you.

Example: Base word: violin

Definition: one who plays the violin

Word with suffix: violinist

27. Base word: starve

Definition: the condition of not having enough to eat

Word with suffix: _____

28. Base word: fame

Definition: having fame or being known by many people

Word with suffix: _____

29. Base word: friend

Definition: the state of being friends

Word with suffix: _____

30. Base word: locate

Definition: the state of being located

Word with suffix: _____

31. Base word: educate

Definition: one who educates or teaches

Word with suffix: _____

32. Base word: victory

Definition: having victory or triumph

Word with suffix: _____

© 2009 K12 Inc. All rights reserved.

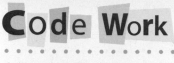

Name:

/oi/ and Suffix –*ology*

Word Sort

Write each word in the box in the correct column below, according to the spelling of the /o/ sound.

destroy	rejoice	joint	avoid	decoy
point	soil	loyal	enjoy	boil
choice	employ	toy	boy	voice

/oi/ Spelled *oi*   /oi/ Spelled *oy*

_____ _____   _____ _____

_____ _____   _____ _____

_____ _____   _____ _____

_____ _____   _____ _____

Choose three words from the box above. On the lines provided below, write a sentence using each word.

1. _____

_____

2. _____

_____

3. _____

_____

© 2009 K12 Inc. All rights reserved.

Using the Suffix –*ology*

The suffix –*ology* means "the study of." Choose a word from the box to match each definition. Write each word on the line provided in the second column.

Hint: The root *anthrop* means "human or man."

geology	biology	zoology
climatology	musicology	anthropology

1. the study of music _____

2. the study of plants and animals _____
(living things)

3. the study of the development _____
of humankind

4. the study of the history of the _____
earth as recorded in rocks

5. the study of different climates _____

6. the study of animals _____

© 2009 K12 Inc. All rights reserved.

Get Ready

■ Verbs must always agree in number with their subject. The subject of a sentence is usually a noun or a pronoun. Below, the different types of subjects are shown with the form of the verb *be* that agrees in number with each subject.

Subject	Example	Verb *be*	
		Present Tense	Past Tense
first person singular pronoun	I	am	was
first person plural pronoun	We	are	were
second person singular pronoun	You	are	were
second person plural pronoun	You	are	were
third person singular pronoun	He/She	is	was
third person plural pronoun	They	are	were
singular noun	The ball	is	was
plural noun	The balls	are	were

■ Another example is the verb *do*.

Subject	Example	Verb *do*	
		Present Tense	Past Tense
first person singular pronoun	I	do, don't	did, didn't
first person plural pronoun	We	do, don't	did, didn't
second person singular pronoun	You	do, don't	did, didn't
second person plural pronoun	You	do, don't	did, didn't
third person singular pronoun	He/She	does, doesn't	did, didn't
third person plural pronoun	They	do, don't	did, didn't
singular noun	The ball	does, doesn't	did, didn't
plural noun	The balls	do, don't	did, didn't

© 2009 K12 Inc. All rights reserved.

Try It

Underline the correct verb form of the word pair in parentheses.
The subject of each sentence is shown in **bold**.

1. **I** (has, have) a big, brown dog.

2. **We** (is, are) taking him to the dog park today.

3. **He** (love, loves) to play with other dogs.

4. **They** (fetch, fetches) sticks when we throw them.

5. Sometimes, **we** (play, plays) catch with a ball.

6. **The dogs** (don't, doesn't) fight over the ball—they (take, takes) turns!

7. **I** (am, are) looking forward to the dog park!

© 2009 K12 Inc. All rights reserved.

Name: _____

Mystery Words

Choose a word from the box to match each clue below. Write each word on the line provided in the second column. Underline the letters in each word that make the /oi/ sound, and then read each word aloud.

enjoy	soil	voice	boy	moist	joy	destroy

Clue	Word
1. to ruin or wreck	_____
2. dirt	_____
3. like very much	_____
4. slightly wet	_____
5. what you use to speak or sing	_____
6. happiness	_____
7. opposite of girl	_____

Choose three words from the box above. On the lines provided below, write a sentence that uses each word.

8. _____

_____

9. _____

_____

10. _____

_____

© 2009 K12 Inc. All rights reserved.

Using the Suffix *–ive*

The suffix *–ive* means "full of" or "tending toward" an action. Choose a word from the box to match each phrase below. Write each word on the line provided in the second column.

active	destructive	constructive
supportive	instructive	protective

Phrase	**Word**
1. tending toward protection or safety	_____
2. tending toward or full of action and movement	_____
3. tending toward destruction; tearing down, or ruining	_____
4. tending toward construction, or building up	_____
5. full of material for instruction	_____
6. tending toward or full of support	_____

Choose three words from the box above. On the lines provided below, write a sentence that uses each word.

7. _____

_____

8. _____

_____

9. _____

_____

© 2009 K12 Inc. All rights reserved.

Toy Chest of Memories

It was time for spring cleaning and Carl had made up his mind. This was the year he would finally tackle his toy chest. It had been sitting untouched in the corner of his room for years. He had recently heard about a charity group that collected toys for kids. He thought that giving his toys to that group was a *even looked in this*

© 2009 K12 Inc. All rights reserved.

© 2009 K12 Inc. All rights reserved.

to watch you play with those toys. They made you so happy for such a long time. I know they'll do the same for others." Carl sat next to his dad and told him about each toy in the bag. They both smiled at the memories the toys brought back. They made a plan to drop off Carl's bag the next day. They knew the only thing better than thinking about the days Carl played with the toys was to see other children enjoying the toys just as much.

thing in years, Carl thought. *Who knows what I'll find inside?*

Carl opened the lid. He was instantly struck with memories. The toy on top was a plastic cowboy. Carl wiggled the cowboy's arms and chuckled. "I can't believe I forgot about you," Carl said to the cowboy, as if the cowboy could hear him. "You remind me of my cowboy phase. I used to want nothing more than to grow up to be a cowboy. I wouldn't leave the house without my cowboy boots. I always had to have my cowboy hat, too." Carl put the cowboy in the donation bag. "You'll make some kid really happy," he said.

When Carl reached in the toy chest again, he heard a soft squeak. As soon as the noise reached his ears, Carl knew

© 2009 K12 Inc. All rights reserved.

"I know," Carl replied. "I haven't played with these toys in years. I thought it would be a good idea to give them to some kids who don't have many toys."

"That's a great idea, Carl," his dad agreed. "It used to bring me great joy

© 2009 K12 Inc. All rights reserved.

exactly what it was. "Ha! That squeaking used to follow me everywhere!" Carl said as he pulled a stuffed animal from the chest. "My family used to listen for the squeak to know where I was in the

© 2009 K12 Inc. All rights reserved.

---

to buy. Then I would ring up their items and give them their total. They would pretend to give me money. Then I would give them coins for change. This cash register and these coins even helped me learn to count money," Carl said. "It's time to pass you on. Now you can help another kid learn to count money."

By the time Carl had finished emptying his toy chest, his donation bag was full. He picked it up to take to his dad. As Carl carried it, his dad heard the squeaks, voices, and other noises coming from the toys. His dad smiled. "I recognize those sounds," he said. "I haven't heard them since you were a little boy."

© 2009 K12 Inc. All rights reserved.

© 2009 K12 Inc. All rights reserved.

house." Carl looked at the animal and smiled. He pulled off the bandages and makeshift cast. "I used to dream of working with animals. I thought I might be a vet," he said. "I performed more surgeries on this stuffed animal than I can remember. Guess it's time for you to squeak for someone else." Carl placed the squeaky animal in the bag with his old cowboy.

After pulling out a few more toys from his toy chest, Carl heard a faint voice. "Oh, I'd recognize that voice anywhere!" Carl exclaimed. "This doll was by my side for months! After I decided against working with animals, I thought I'd try my hand at being a children's doctor. This poor doll has survived enough

© 2009 K12 Inc. All rights reserved.

cuts and scrapes to last a lifetime," he recalled. "I'm sure you'll enjoy living with another kid," Carl said to the doll. "One who won't poke and prod you all the time!" Then he added her to the growing bag of old toys.

Carl dug through the toy chest for most of the day. When he finally reached the bottom, he saw a handful of plastic coins. Next to the coins sat a plastic cash register. Carl pulled out the register. Then he grabbed the coins. He pushed the buttons on the register and listened to the noises they made. He opened the cash register's drawer and put the coins inside. "I played with this when I wanted to work at a grocery store. I would ask my parents what they wanted

/ou/ and Suffix –eer

Word Sort

Write each word in the box in the correct column below, according to that word's spelling of the /ou/ sound. Then write two new words for each spelling of the /ou/ sound.

| bounce | now | chowder | grouch | proud | town |
| discount | without | pouch | crown | growl | frown |

/ou/ Spelled *ou*   **/ou/ Spelled *ow***

_____   _____

_____   _____

_____   _____

_____   _____

_____   _____

New: _____   **New:** _____

New: _____   **New:** _____

Choose one word from each spelling of the /ou/ sound above. On the lines provided below, write a sentence using each word.

1. _____

_____

2. _____

_____

© 2009 K12 Inc. All rights reserved.

Using the Suffix *–eer*

The suffix *–eer* means "one who uses or conducts." Choose a word from the box to match each phrase below. Write each word on the lines provided.
Hint: Two words in the box will not be used.

puppeteer	musketeer	engineer	rocketeer
electioneer	auctioneer	balladeer	mountaineer

Phrase   **Word**

1. one who fires, pilots, or rides in a rocket   _____

2. one who plans and builds roads,   _____
   buildings, or machines

3. one who uses puppets   _____

4. one who sells items at a public sale   _____
   to those who offer to pay the most

5. one who works to help get a   _____
   candidate elected

6. one who lives in or climbs mountains   _____

Use a dictionary to look up the two words from the box above that were
not used. Write each word and its definition on the lines provided below.

7. Word: _____

   Definition: _____

8. Word: _____

   Definition: _____

© 2009 K12 Inc. All rights reserved.

/ou/ Spelled *ou* and *ow*

Underline the letters that make the /ou/ sound in each word. Then write each word in a sentence on the line provided below. The first one has been done for you.

Hint: A scoundrel is "a mean person."

1. Word: cr<u>ow</u>d

   Sentence: When the singer came onstage, the crowd went wild.

2. Word: allow

   Sentence: _____

3. Word: blouse

   Sentence: _____

4. Word: scoundrel

   Sentence: _____

5. Word: frown

   Sentence: _____

6. Word: sound

   Sentence: _____

7. Word: now

   Sentence: _____

8. Word: mouse

   Sentence: _____

9. Word: couch

   Sentence: _____

10. Word: down

    Sentence: _____

© 2009 K12 Inc. All rights reserved.

Using the Suffix –*ess*

The suffix –*ess* makes a noun feminine. Choose a word from the box to match each definition below. Write each word in the second column on the lines provided next to the definitions.

| actress | hostess | waitress | countess | seamstress |

Definition   **Word**

1. a woman who lives in a grand old castle _____

2. a woman who serves food in a restaurant _____

3. a woman who sews clothes and fixes seams _____

4. a woman who holds a party _____

5. a woman who performs in a movie _____

Choose three words from the box above. On the lines provided below., write a sentence that uses each word.

6. _____

_____

7. _____

_____

8. _____

_____

© 2009 K12 Inc. All rights reserved.

In the Clouds

Vince plopped down on the couch next to his cousin Fay. "I'm bored," he growled.

"Join the club. I don't think I've ever been this bored in my life," Fay groaned with a frown.

"The television is broken. We've played all of the board games in the house. We've flipped through all of the

© 2009 K12 Inc. All rights reserved.

"You're right," Vince agreed. "I guess that means tomorrow we should look for people and buildings in the clouds."

Their uncle smiled. He knew a beautiful day and their imaginations were all Fay and Vince needed to have fun.

© 2009 K12 nc. All rights reserved.

magazines a hundred times. There's nothing else to do," Vince grumbled.

"Don't you think you're giving up a little early?" asked Paul, their uncle.

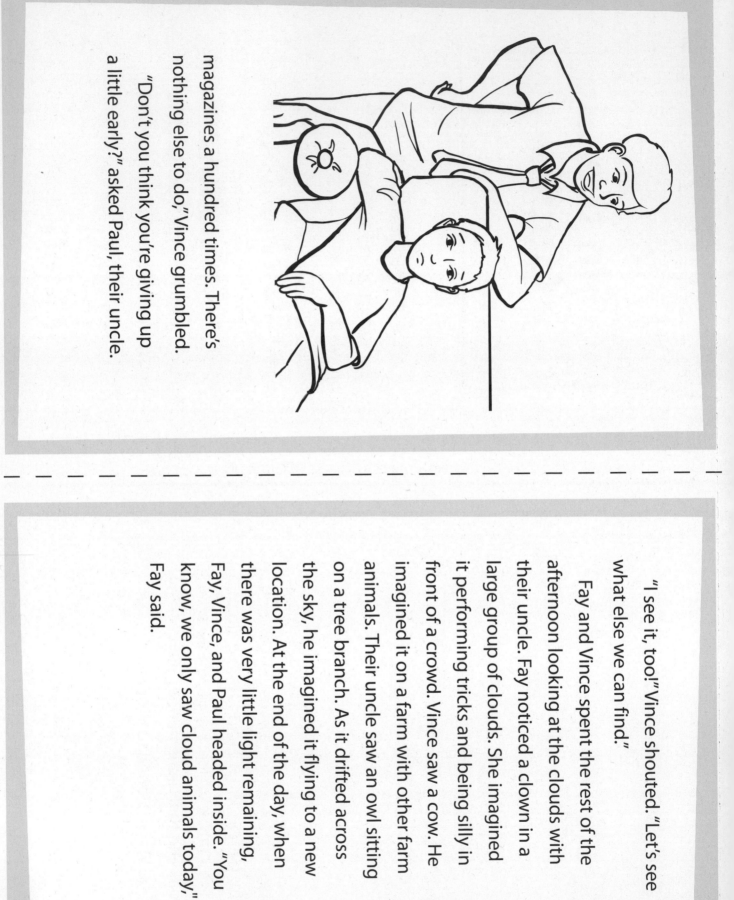

© 2009 K12 Inc. All rights reserved.

"I see it, too!" Vince shouted. "Let's see what else we can find."

Fay and Vince spent the rest of the afternoon looking at the clouds with their uncle. Fay noticed a clown in a large group of clouds. She imagined it performing tricks and being silly in front of a crowd. Vince saw a cow. He imagined it on a farm with other farm animals. Their uncle saw an owl sitting on a tree branch. As it drifted across the sky, he imagined it flying to a new location. At the end of the day, when there was very little light remaining, Fay, Vince, and Paul headed inside. "You know, we only saw cloud animals today," Fay said.

© 2009 K12 Inc. All rights reserved.

"Everything I heard you mention is something you can do indoors. It sounds like you haven't even considered what you could do outside."

"Vince's bat broke when we were playing with it yesterday," Fay replied.

"Our kites are a tangled mess," Vince added.

"What about your imaginations? Are those broken, too?" Paul asked. "When I was your age, I didn't have all of the games and toys you have now. That didn't matter. You would have never caught me sitting inside on the couch on such a nice day. I certainly wouldn't complain about not having anything fun to do."

© 2009 K12 Inc. All rights reserved.

imagination time to warm up. Let me see if I can spot something in the clouds," Paul replied. He scanned the sky and then pointed his finger. "Look, do you see that small group of clouds over there?"

Fay and Vince followed his finger with their gazes. "Yes, but it doesn't look like anything to me. All I see are regular clouds," Vince said.

"Well, I see something in those clouds. I see a mouse. It has a small face with two round ears. I can even see whiskers. It looks like the mouse is nibbling on a wedge of cheese," Paul said.

"Hmm, I don't see that," Fay said. "Wait, yes I do! I see a mouse, too! Can you see it, Vince?"

© 2009 K12 Inc. All rights reserved.

"Well, what did you use to do for fun?" Fay asked.

"On nice days like today, I would spread a blanket on the ground outside. Then I would lie down and look up at the sky. I'd look for as many cloud figures I could find," Paul answered.

"Cloud figures? What're those?" Vince asked.

"Cloud figures are what I saw when I used my imagination and looked at the clouds. Sometimes the clouds looked like animals. Sometimes I thought they looked like buildings. As the figures floated across the sky, it was almost like I was watching a movie," Paul said. "Would you like to give it a try?"

© 2009 K12 Inc. All rights reserved.

"Well, we don't really have anything else to do," Fay replied.

"We may as well give it a shot," Vince added. Paul could tell that Fay and Vince were not excited about his plan. However, he was convinced that a little time using their imaginations would change their minds.

After several minutes of lying outside, Fay was ready to give up. "We've been out here for hours and we still haven't seen one animal, person, or building in the clouds. Let's go back inside," she said, pouting.

"Fay, it's only been a few minutes, not hours. You have to give your

© 2009 K12 Inc. All rights reserved.

Mystery Words

Choose a word from the box to match each clue below. Write that word in the second column on the line provided. Then read aloud each word that you write.

furnace	surface	terrace	notice
practice	palace	novice	necklace

Clue	**Word**
1. a big, fancy castle	_____
2. somebody who is new at something	_____
3. jewelry you wear around your neck	_____
4. to become aware of something	_____
5. doing something a lot to get better at it	_____
6. it puts out a lot of heat	_____
7. a flat platform outside a house	_____
8. the top of a body of water	_____

© 2009 K12 Inc. All rights reserved.

Prefix Practice

Add the suffix –ical to each word and write the new words on the lines provided. The first one has been done for you as an example.

1. history   _historical_

2. biology   _____

3. angel   _____

4. alphabet   _____

5. cosmology _____

6. psychology _____

7. graph _____

8. mythology _____

Choose three of the words you created above and write a sentence that uses each word on the lines provided below.

9. Word: _____

Sentence: _____

_____

10. Word: _____

Sentence: _____

_____

11. Word: _____

Sentence: _____

_____

© 2009 K12 Inc. All rights reserved.

Unit 4 Assessment

Part 1.

Listen to each sound as it is read to you. Circle the group or groups of letters that can make each sound that you hear.

1. oi   ou   ow   oy   ace   ice
2. oi   ou   ow   oy   ace   ice
3. oi   ou   ow   oy   ace   ice
4. oi   ou   ow   oy   ace   ice
5. oi   ou   ow   oy   ace   ice
6. oi   ou   ow   oy   ace   ice
7. oi   ou   ow   oy   ace   ice
8. oi   ou   ow   oy   ace   ice
9. oi   ou   ow   oy   ace   ice

Part 2.

Read each word in the box. Then write each word under the correct heading in the chart below, according to the spelling at the top of each column. The first one in each column has been done for you.

office	palace	coil	decoy	necklace	moist
chow	frown	mound	crowd	joyful	notice

10.   /oi/   **11.**   /ou/   **12.**   /us/

decoy _____   frown _____   office _____

_____   _____   _____

_____   _____   _____

_____   _____   _____

© 2009 K12 Inc. All rights reserved.

Part 3.

In each sentence below, underline any word that contains the /oi/, /ou/, or /us/ sound.

13. I did not notice the brown dog until he let out a howl.

14. The queen wore a crown to the event at the palace.

15. The boy took photos during his visit to the town.

16. I went to join the crowd outside on the terrace.

17. Roy found a necklace on the ground.

Part 4.

Listen to each word as it is read to you. On the line provided, write the word that you hear.

18. _____   24. _____

19. _____   25. _____

20. _____   26. _____

21. _____   27. _____

22. _____   28. _____

23. _____   29. _____

© 2009 K12 Inc. All rights reserved.

Part 5.

Read each definition below. Then select the correct word from the second line to match each definition, and write that word on the line provided below.

30. Definition: one who lives in or climbs mountains

    Choices: mountaineer, mountainous, mountains

    Answer: ⸻

31. Definition: a woman or girl who performs in plays, movies, or television shows

    Choices: active, actress, acts

    Answer: ⸻

32. Definition: funny or amusing

    Choices: comic, comical, comics

    Answer: ⸻

33. Definition: relating or pertaining to the imagination

    Choices: imaginary, imaginations, imagine

    Answer: ⸻

34. Definition: the study of the history, forms, and methods of music

    Choices: music, musical, musicology

    Answer: ⸻

35. Definition: tending toward safety

    Choices: protective, protector, protects

    Answer: ⸻

© 2009 K12 Inc. All rights reserved.

Part 6.

Read each base word below and then read the definition on the next line. Then add to each base word the correct suffix that matches the definition, and write the new word on the line provided. An example has been done for you.

Example: Base word: zoo

Definition: the study of animal life

Answer: _zoology_____

36. Base word: act

Definition: tending toward or full of actions or movement

Answer: _____

37. Base word: puppet

Definition: one who uses puppets

Answer: _____

38. Base word: host

Definition: a woman who entertains guests or welcomes patrons to a restaurant

Answer: _____

39. Base word: alphabet

Definition: arranged in the order of the alphabet

Answer: _____

40. Base word: custom

Definition: according to custom

Answer: _____

© 2009 K12 Inc. All rights reserved.

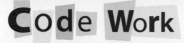

Find the Word

Look up each word in a dictionary. Write your own definition for each word on the lines provided.

1. breakable

Definition: _____

_____

2. divisible

Definition: _____

_____

3. adaptable

Definition: _____

_____

4. knowledgeable

Definition: _____

_____

5. permissible

Definition: _____

_____

Choose two of the words from above. On the lines provided below, write a sentence using each word.

6. Word: _____

Sentence: _____

_____

7. Word: _____

Sentence: _____

_____

© 2009 K12 Inc. All rights reserved.

Name:

able/ible and Suffix –ant

Name That Word!

The suffix –ant means "a person who does something." Add the suffix –ant to the words in the box to make new words that fit the clues below. Write each new word on the line provided next to the clue. Remember, sometimes a base word's spelling changes when you add the suffix –ant.

account	consult	attend
serve	participate	apply

Clue	**Word**
1. a person who applies to join a group	_____
2. a person who attends to, or takes care of, an area	_____
3. a person who accounts for, or keeps track of, money	_____
4. a person with whom you consult for advice on a problem	_____
5. a person you pay to do household chores	_____
6. a person who participates in, or takes part in, an event	_____

© 2009 K12 Inc. All rights reserved.

Add the Ending

Read each word in the box aloud. Add the correct ending, *–able* or *–ible*, to each word and write the word in the correct column below.

| comfort | reduce | depend | suggest | corrupt |
| change | mistake | believe | notice | admit |

Words Ending in *–ible*

_____

_____

_____

_____

Words Ending in *–able*

_____

_____

_____

_____

_____

_____

Choose three of the *–able* or *–ible* words above. Write a sentence using each word.

1. _____

   _____

2. _____

   _____

3. _____

   _____

© 2009 K12 Inc. All rights reserved.

Word Work

Name:

able/ible **and Suffix** *–worthy*

Complete the Sentence

The suffix *–worthy* means "fit for or deserving." Read each word in the chart and its definition. Choose a word to complete each sentence below. Write that word on the line provided.

Word	Meaning
newsworthy	worth putting in the news
seaworthy	fit to go to sea
trustworthy	worthy of one's trust
noteworthy	worth taking special note of
airworthy	fit to fly
roadworthy	fit to drive on the road

1. I will tell you my secret because you are a _____ person.

2. The airplane needed to get its engine fixed before it would be _____ .

3. This boat may be ugly, but it is _____ and safe.

4. The reporter was looking for a _____ story.

5. The old car needed new tires before it would be _____ .

6. It was _____ that I could hear air leaking from my bike's tire.

© 2009 K12 Inc. All rights reserved.

A Puppy for Paige

"Aw, he looks so cute!" Paige cried out to her mother as she looked down at the scruffy puppy on their porch. "Can we keep him? Please, please, please!" she begged.

"Well, I guess he'll need somewhere to stay while we look for his owners. I'm not saying you can keep him forever, but you can keep him for now," her mother answered.

© 2009 K12 Inc. All rights reserved.

---

good care of my puppy," she said to Paige. "Your mother tells me you've been very dependable while caring for Scooter. If you're interested, I could use a trustworthy person to walk him twice a day while I'm at work. Is that something you'd like to do?"

"I'd love to!" Paige exclaimed. "I guess if I can't keep him for myself, seeing him every day is the next best thing. Thanks!" Paige handed over Scooter with a smile. She was happy to know that Scooter had a nice home, and that he would still be a part of her life.

© 2009 K12 Inc. All rights reserved.

© 2009 K12 Inc. All rights reserved.

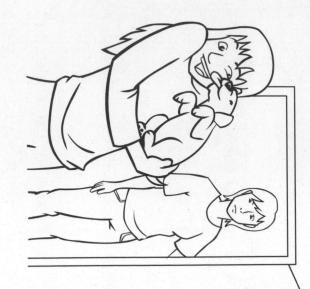

Paige reached down and scooped up the puppy. He licked Paige's face. Paige giggled at the lovable puppy. He was wagging his tail so hard and fast, it made it difficult for Paige to hold him. "I think you're just as excited as I am," she

---

© 2009 K12 Inc. All rights reserved.

puppy. I'm sorry," her mother answered. Paige looked over at the puppy. He looked so comfortable in their house. How could she give him back?

"I guess it's time to find out once and for all," Paige said. "Scooter, here boy." The puppy jumped up and ran over to her. "Maybe he was just responding to the sound of my voice," Paige reasoned.

"There's only one way to find out," her mother replied. "Check behind his ear." Paige looked behind the puppy's left ear. It was small, but there was definitely an unmistakable mark there. Paige looked crushed.

Paige's mother picked up the phone to call Scooter's owner. When she arrived, his owner looked very relieved. "Thank you so much for taking such said to the puppy. Paige played with him until he looked tired. Then she grabbed an old blanket and placed it on the floor in the corner of her bedroom. "You can sleep in my room," she said. As if he understood her, the puppy followed Paige to the blanket and plopped down. He was asleep in minutes. Paige went to join her mother in the living room.

"I know you really want to keep the puppy, Paige, but we need to try to find his owners. It's the right thing to do," her mother said.

"I know. It's just that I've wanted a puppy since I was a little girl. You always said when I was older and more responsible, you'd consider letting me have one. Maybe this is the puppy for me," Paige replied.

© 2009 K12 Inc. All rights reserved.

---

owner? Maybe she just wants a puppy and saw that we found one," Paige reasoned.

"She said the puppy answers to the name Scooter. She also said he has an unmistakable mark behind his left ear. If we find that mark, we have to return the

© 2009 K12 Inc. All rights reserved.

"Let's see how the next few days go. We'll make flyers and post them. If no one comes for the puppy, and you've proven that you can take good care of him, I'll let you keep him," her mother decided.

"Thank you, thank you, thank you!" Paige exclaimed. "I'll prove to you that I'm responsible. I'll feed and water him. I'll walk him twice a day. I'll play with him all the time. You'll see. I'll be the most dependable pet owner ever!"

The next morning, Paige took the puppy for a walk. When she returned home, her mother was sitting at the kitchen table. She had paper and markers in front of her. "I know you don't want to, but we need to make

© 2009 K12 Inc. All rights reserved.

flyers. Someone may be looking for this puppy," she explained. Paige knew her mother was right. They spent the rest of the afternoon making and posting flyers. When they returned home, Paige played with the puppy, took him for a walk, and then fed and watered him. After dinner, she played with the puppy until it was time for bed.

The next morning, Paige took the puppy for another walk. When she returned home, she looked at her mother and could tell something was wrong. "I just received a phone call, Paige. It seems the puppy's owner saw one of our flyers. She's been looking for him for two days," her mother replied.

"How do we know she's really the

© 2009 K12 Inc. All rights reserved.

Get Ready

▪ A **subject** is a noun or pronoun that a sentence is about.
A **direct object** is a noun or pronoun that receives the action of an action verb in a sentence.

Mom called Dad.

Subject: Mom

Verb: called

Direct object: Dad

Transitive verbs pass the action from the subject to the direct object. In the sentence above, the word *called* is a transitive verb.

▪ Notice in the sentence, "Grandpa yelled," that there is no direct object. When there is no direct object, the verb is an **intransitive verb**.

Grandpa yelled.

Subject: Grandpa

Verb: yelled

▪ With intransitive verbs, there is always a subject, but never a direct object. Why not? The sentence may...

...not name any direct object.

Example: *Bob was reading.*

...not need a direct object to make sense.

Example: *I ran.*

...not have an action for a direct object.

Example: *She is tired.*

© 2009 K12 Inc. All rights reserved.

Try It

Underline the verb in each sentence. If the verb is transitive, write "T" on the line provided. If the verb is intransitive, write "I" on the line provided.

1. The women chatted loudly. _____

2. The boys argued about the game. _____

3. Bob called Jim. _____

4. Betsy is very happy today. _____

5. The hikers rested by the water. _____

6. The cop stopped the speeding car. _____

7. Dean ate all the candy. _____

8. The fireman climbed the ladder. _____

9. Mary sneezed. _____

© 2009 K12 Inc. All rights reserved.

Verb-to-Noun with –*ion*

The base words given below are verbs. Change the base words into nouns by adding the correct suffix according to the rules below.

Rule 1: When a base word ends in *t*, add the suffix –*ion*.

Rule 2: When a base word ends in *te*, drop the *e* and add –*ion*.

Rule 3: When a base word ends in *d*, drop the *d* and add –*sion*.

Rule 4: When a base word ends in *de*, drop the *de* and add –*sion*.

Write each new word on the line provided.

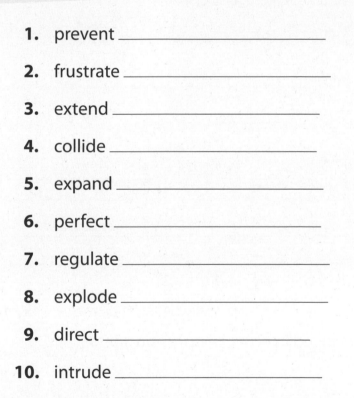

1. prevent _____

2. frustrate _____

3. extend _____

4. collide _____

5. expand _____

6. perfect _____

7. regulate _____

8. explode _____

9. direct _____

10. intrude _____

© 2009 K12 Inc. All rights reserved.

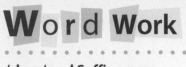
/shun/ and Suffix –*some*

The suffix –*some*

The suffix –*some* can mean "tending to be." On the lines provided, write the word with the suffix –*some* that matches each definition given. The first one has been done for you as an example.

1. tending to be feared <u>fearsome</u>

2. tending to be a bother _____

3. tending to inspire awe _____

4. tending to be trouble _____

5. tending to be a burden _____

6. tending to be tiring _____

New Vocabulary!

Below are three words and their definitions. Read the definitions, choose the word that best completes each sentence, and write that word on the line provided.

Word	Meaning
adventuresome	tending to take risks or enjoy new things
cumbersome	tending to be difficult to move, especially because of size or weight
meddlesome	tending to get involved in other people's business

7. Beth is so _____ ! She always wants to know things that are none of her business.

8. Moving the refrigerator was _____ . It took three of us just to get it through the door.

9. You are so _____ ! I would never have the courage to go white-water rafting.

© 2009 K12 Inc. All rights reserved.

Winning Friends

Nate was excited when he saw the sign. He pedaled his bike as fast as he could to get home. "Mom! Dad! Guess what I just saw," he yelled as he walked in the front door. "The recreation center down the street is having a day of competitions. That would be a great way for me to make new friends!" He took a few minutes to catch his breath before

© 2009 K12 Inc. All rights reserved.

competition and tell the truth. I'll go with you if you'd like," she offered.

"No thanks. I got myself into this mess. I'll do what it takes to get out of it," Nate replied. He spent the next few minutes explaining the situation to each person he played. He was really worried they would all hate him and never speak to him again. The funny thing was, each person started off upset, but they all forgave Nate. They all still wanted to be his friend. That day, Nate realized that some things were more important than winning. Some things, like honesty and courage, were what friends valued most.

© 2009 K12 Inc. All rights reserved

© 2009 K12 Inc. All rights reserved.

continuing. "We haven't lived here long, so the timing is perfect. Maybe I won't have to spend my summer all alone after all."

Nate's parents were happy for him. They'd watched him mope around their old house for weeks before they moved. Then they'd watched him mope around their new house for the past few weeks since they'd moved here. "That's great news, Nate," his father said. "You've been unhappy for a while now, so it's good to see you excited about something."

"I agree. We haven't seen you smile in quite some time. This day of competitions may be just what you need to change your mind about the move," his mother added.

© 2009 K12 Inc. All rights reserved.

how he won the competition. Ms. Lee could tell by looking at Nate that he felt bad. "Well, after hearing your confession, I must say I'm disappointed. However, you did tell the truth. That took courage. I know that wasn't easy to do. I think you need to talk to each person in your

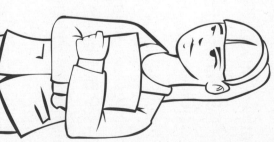

That weekend, Nate rode his bike to the recreation center. He arrived just as the center director was explaining the day's events. "First you'll choose from a

© 2009 K12 Inc. All rights reserved.

After an hour of instruction, it was time for the competition. Nate played each round the same way. First he let the other player take the lead. Then he'd come from behind to win. After each victory, Nate smiled and pretended he had just been lucky. However, with each win, Nate felt worse and worse. He realized that he didn't like winning this way. He was cheating and it wasn't right. After the last match, Nate made a decision. He would tell the director the truth.

"Ms. Lee, I have a confession to make," Nate said.

"What do you mean, Nate?" she asked. Nate told Ms. Lee about his plan and

© 2009 K12 Inc. All rights reserved.

list of events. We've included checkers, chess, table tennis, and basketball. Then the instructors and I will spend an hour teaching you your activity. We ask that you choose an activity that is new to you. That way, everyone is at the same skill level when it's time for the competitions later this afternoon. Are there any questions?" asked the director, Ms. Lee. No one had any questions. Everyone was ready to get started!

Nate looked around the room. He was happy to see so many boys and girls his age. Nate knew this was his chance to make friends in his new town, and he knew just how to do it. *Everyone likes a winner. I'll sign up for chess and*

pretend like I've never played before today. Everyone will be so impressed with how well I play. Winning the competition will win me friends, for sure! he thought to himself. Then he walked over to the registration table to sign up.

During the hour of instruction, Nate did a nice job of acting as if he'd never played chess. Sometimes he made incorrect moves. Other times he let other players collect some of his pieces. The instructor told Nate several times that he was a good player. The other players asked him how he could remember all the rules so quickly. Nate just smiled and shrugged his shoulders.

© 2009 K12 Inc. All rights reserved.

© 2009 K12 Inc. All rights reserved.

/shun/ and /zhun/

The base words below are verbs. Review the rules for adding the suffix –*sion* to base words.

Rule 1: When a base word ends in –*ss*, add the letters *ion*. The final syllable becomes –*sion*, pronounced /shun/.

Rule 2: When a base word ends in the /z/ sound, drop the letters that make the /z/ sound and add *sion*. The final syllable becomes –*sion*, pronounced /zhun/.

Rewrite each verb as a noun, on the line provided, by using the suffix –*sion*.

1. possess   possession _____

2. supervise   _____

3. confess   _____

4. progress   _____

5. televise   _____

6. discuss   _____

All of the following words end in either –*tion* or –*sion*. Read each word aloud. Underline the sound made by that word's final syllable.

7. revision (/shun/, /zhun/)   12. collision (/shun/, /zhun/)

8. impression (/shun/, /zhun/)   13. perfection (/shun/, /zhun/)

9. profession (/shun/, /zhun/)   14. extension (/shun/, /zhun/)

10. celebration (/shun/, /zhun/)   15. exclusion (/shun/, /zhun/)

11. intrusion (/shun/, /zhun/)

© 2009 K12 Inc. All rights reserved.

Name: _____

Searching for –ish

Find and circle each word from the box in the word search chart below.
Words may appear across, down, or backward.

childish	sluggish	darkish	thirtyish
boyish	babyish	reddish	yellowish

b	a	b	y	i	s	h	h	s	t
o	h	c	d	d	b	s	a	i	h
y	c	h	i	l	d	i	s	h	i
i	h	i	s	g	g	d	i	c	r
s	s	c	h	s	h	d	b	h	t
h	i	g	i	d	y	e	b	i	y
k	w	h	s	i	k	r	a	d	i
d	o	h	s	i	g	g	u	l	s
i	l	u	h	a	d	k	r	i	h
s	l	l	y	e	l	o	w	b	r
h	e	s	d	l	i	d	c	a	e
r	y	d	a	i	s	h	a	b	d

© 2009 K12 Inc. All rights reserved.

Get Ready

◾ Some words are easy to confuse because they sound exactly the same—*write* and *right*, or *to, two,* and *too.*

◾ Other words get mixed up because they sound similar or because they are closely related. Let's look at some pairs of words that can be easy to confuse.

Let and Leave

Let means "to permit or to allow."

I *let* Jack help me.

Leave means "to depart, or go without taking."

I will *leave* my coat at home.

Teach and Learn

Teach means "to give instruction."

I will *teach* you long division.

Learn means "to receive instruction."

Someday, I will *learn* to drive.

Good and Well

Good tells "what kind."

Jan is a *good* soccer player.

What is Jan? A *good* soccer player.

Well tells "how."

Jan plays soccer *well*.

How does Jan play? *Well*.

Real and Very

Real means "genuine or true."

I like to cook with *real* butter.

Very means "extremely."

I was *very* tired.

© 2009 K12 Inc. All rights reserved.

Try It

Underline the correct word in parentheses to complete each sentence below.

1. I will (teach, learn) you about making bread.

2. When you make bread, you must (let, leave) the dough rise.

3. Letting the dough rise is a (real, very) important step.

4. If you skip this step, the bread won't turn out (good, well).

In each pair of words below, cross out the word that you used above. Use the remaining word in a sentence. Write sentences on the lines provided.

5. teach, learn

_____

_____

6. let, leave

_____

_____

7. real, very

_____

_____

8. good, well

_____

_____

© 2009 K12 Inc. All rights reserved.

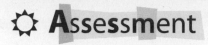
able/ible & /shun/ and Suffixes

Unit 5 Assessment

Part 1.

Listen to each word as it is read to you. Write each word on the line provided.

1. _____

2. _____

3. _____

4. _____

5. _____

6. _____

7. _____

8. _____

Part 2.

Write each word from the box in the correct column below, according to the sound made by its final syllable, /shun/ or /zhun/.

9.

profession	suspension	intrusion	correction
calculation	exclusion	collision	

/shun/   **/zhun/**

_____   _____

_____   _____

_____   _____

_____   _____

© 2009 K12 Inc. All rights reserved.

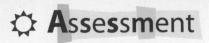

Assessment

Name: _____

Part 3.

Listen to each word as it is read to you. Write each word on the line provided.

10. _____

11. _____

12. _____

13. _____

14. _____

15. _____

Part 4.

Read the sentences below. Underline *true* if the spelling rule is correct;
underline *false* if the spelling rule is incorrect.

16. When a word ends in soft *c*, keep the silent *e* and add –*able*. (true, false)

17. When a word ends in soft *g*, drop the silent *e* and add –*able*. (true, false)

18. Words that end in –*ible* can also end in /shun/. (true, false)

19. When a word ends in silent *e*, keep the *e* and add –*able*. (true, false)

© 2009 K12 Inc. All rights reserved.

Part 5.

Read each definition and select the correct word to match the definition. Write the word on the line provided below.

20. Definition: someone who is deserving of praise

Choices: praised, praising, praiseworthy

Answer: _____

21. Definition: in the direction of the sky

Choices: skyline, skyward, skydive

Answer: _____

22. Definition: tending to be a bother

Choices: bothering, bothered, bothersome

Answer: _____

23. Definition: similar to a fool

Choices: foolish, fooling, fooled

Answer: _____

24. Definition: someone who consults

Choices: consultant, consulting, consultation

Answer: _____

25. Definition: a group with four members

Choices: fourthly, foursome, fourfold

Answer: _____

© 2009 K12 Inc. All rights reserved.

Part 6.

Choose the word from the box that best completes each sentence below.
Write that word on the line provided.

participant	accountant	sluggish	trustworthy
southern	northward	threesome	

26. I tell Rachel all my secrets because she is very _____ .

27. After a relaxing weekend, I often feel _____ on Monday morning.

28. Cindy is our _____ and does our taxes every April.

29. I am a _____ in this year's town-wide spelling bee.

30. We traveled _____ on Route 95, from Florida to Maine.

31. The band is a _____ ; Blake, Josh, and I are its only members.

32. Louisiana is a _____ state

© 2009 K12 Inc. All rights reserved.

Name: _____

Practice with Plurals

Determine what should be done to each base word to make it plural.
Place a ✓ in the correct column. Write the plural form of the base word
in the final column. The first one has been done for you.

Base Word	To Make the Word Plural		Plural Word
	Add –s	**Change y to i and Add –es**	
valley	✓		valleys
territory			
journey			
diary			
county			
holiday			
library			
turkey			
highway			
country			
tray			
dragonfly			
birthday			
family			
decoy			
cowboy			

© 2009 K12 Inc. All rights reserved.

Plurals and Suffix –dom

Using the Suffix –*dom*

The suffix –*dom* means "the condition of, or domain." Add the suffix –*dom* to each word in box to make new words to fit the meanings below.

free	king	star	bore

Meaning | **Word**

1. the domain or territory ruled by a king _____

2. the condition of being bored or uninterested _____

3. the condition of being free or independent _____

4. the condition of being a star or an outstanding performer _____

On the lines provided below, write a sentence that uses each word created above.

5. _____

_____

6. _____

_____

7. _____

_____

8. _____

_____

© 2009 K12 Inc. All rights reserved.

Name:

Practice with Plurals

In the Singular column, write the singular form of each plural word listed in the Plural column. The first one has been done for you.

Plural	Singular
tomatoes	tomato
loaves	
echoes	
potatoes	
calves	
scarves	
wolves	
shelves	

Choose two plural words from above. Write each word in a sentence on the lines provided below.

1. _____

_____

2. _____

_____

© 2009 K12 Inc. All rights reserved.

Base Word Practice

The base word *act* means "to do or to behave." Add the base word *act* to each prefix or suffix shown below, and write the new word on the line provided. Then write a short definition for each new word.

Hint: The prefix *inter–* means "between or among."

1. *inter–* _____

Definition: _____

2. *–ive* _____

Definition: _____

3. *–or* _____

Definition: _____

4. *–ress* _____

Definition: _____

On the lines provided below, write sentences that use each *act* word you created above.

5. _____

_____

6. _____

_____

7. _____

_____

8. _____

_____

© 2009 K12 Inc. All rights reserved.

Val Lends a Helping Hand

"Well, my day just got a little busier. Nope, let me rephrase that. My day just got incredibly busier!"Val's dad said as he hung up the phone.

"Why do you say that? What's going on?"Val asked.

"That was my assistant on the phone. He's sick and he won't be able to help out with the big party tomorrow. Now I'm stuck preparing for the event all by myself," her dad explained.

© 2009 K12 Inc. All rights reserved.

---

slower, I can start teaching you how to make some of those dishes. Would you like that?" he asked.

"I certainly would!"Val responded.

"Maybe I'll follow in your footsteps. We can make catering a family business," she said with a smile. Val and her dad spent the rest of the afternoon adding the finishing touches to the dishes. Val paid careful attention to each step. She knew it wouldn't be long before she was making them all by herself.

© 2009 K12 Inc. All rights reserved.

© 2009 K12 Inc. All rights reserved.

"You won't have to do it all by yourself. I'll help," Val offered.

"Thanks, Val! I could really use the help. We better get started if we're going to prepare enough food to feed 150

© 2009 K12 Inc. All rights reserved.

time. You seemed to know what needed to be done without my having to ask you. You saved me time and made it possible for me to prepare each dish in less time," her dad replied. "Maybe after the holidays, when things are a little people tomorrow!" her dad responded. Val's dad was a caterer. He was usually pretty busy, but the holidays brought more big parties than any other time of year. Val knew her dad could use her help. She just hoped it was enough to make the party a success.

Val's dad scribbled a list on a piece of paper. "The first thing we need to do is go to the grocery store. My assistant was supposed to pick up a few ingredients on his way over this morning. Since he's not coming, we have to pick them up ourselves," he said.

They made the quick drive to the grocery store. Once there, they grabbed a cart and headed inside. "What can I grab?" Val asked.

© 2009 K12 Inc. All rights reserved.

and silverware. As she let the dishes soak, she watched her dad work. Val had no idea her dad was such a great chef. He sliced, diced, chopped, and mixed the ingredients faster than anyone she'd ever seen. After Val washed and dried the glasses and silverware, she helped her dad measure the ingredients for the next dishes. As her dad finished up the desserts, Val cleaned up the kitchen. By the end of the day, Val and her dad were exhausted, but they were proud, too.

"Thanks for letting me help, Dad. You're a great chef. It was really amazing to watch you in action," she said.

"I should be the one thanking you, Val. Without your help, I don't know if I would have gotten everything done on

© 2009 K12 Inc. All rights reserved.

© 2009 K12 Inc. All rights reserved.

Her dad reviewed the list. "You can get one bag of apples and two bags of potatoes. We also need four loaves of bread, five tomatoes, and eight heads of lettuce. I'll get everything else," her dad replied. Val and her dad set off in different directions. They grabbed the supplies and headed to the cash register. After checking out, they loaded up the car and headed home. During the car ride, Val's dad went over the things they needed to do to prepare for the party. "Let's see. I'll get started on the salads and dressings. Then I'll prepare the potatoes. I'll finish up with the desserts. We made the main courses yesterday, so I think that covers everything," he said.

© 2009 K12 Inc. All rights reserved.

"What can I help you do?" Val asked.

"Oh, I didn't forget about you. I'll need you to wash all of the fruits and vegetables before I use them. I'll also need you to wash all of the glasses and silverware we'll be using for the party. You'll need to be careful. The knives are really sharp. I don't want you to cut yourself," he warned.

When they arrived home, Val and her dad grabbed the bags of groceries and headed straight for the kitchen. They immediately got to work. Val scrubbed every apple, potato, tomato, and head of lettuce she had picked up at the store. She passed each one off to her dad as soon as it was washed. She filled the sink with soap and water to wash the glasses

Practice with Plurals

Read the clues to fill in the words in the crossword.

Across

1. singular of potatoes
2. singular of turkeys
3. plural of county
4. singular of highways
5. singular of valleys
6. plural of calf
7. plural of hobby

Down

8. singular of echoes
9. singular of tomatoes
10. plural of dragonfly
11. plural of wolf
12. plural of leaf

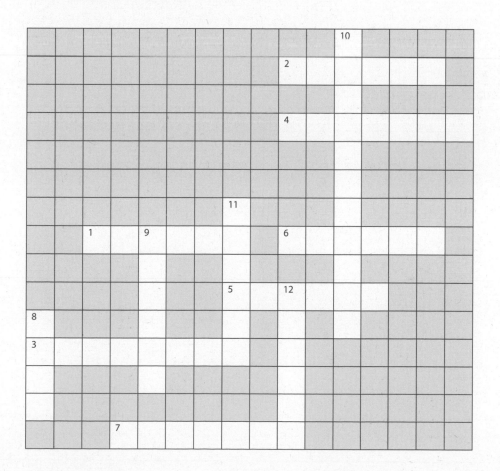

© 2009 K12 Inc. All rights reserved.

Base Word Practice

Unscramble each word and write that word on the line provided. Then write a sentence that uses each word on the lines provided below.

1. eopxrt _____

Definition: to send something to another country to sell it

Sentence: _____

_____

2. iomprt _____

Definition: to bring something in from an outside source

Sentence: _____

_____

3. aeobprlt _____

Definition: able to be carried

Sentence: _____

_____

4. anoprrstt _____

Definition: to carry something across

Sentence: _____

_____

© 2009 K12 Inc. All rights reserved.

Get Ready

■ A *preposition* is a word that relates a noun or a pronoun to some other word in the sentence. The noun or pronoun that follows the preposition is the object of the preposition.

> Shelly went **into** the store.

> (*Store* is the object of the preposition *into*.)

■ A preposition and the noun or pronoun that follows it are separate words, but they do the job of a single modifier. This group of words is called a phrase, and because it begins with a preposition, it is called a *prepositional phrase*.

> Shelly went **into the store**.

■ You use prepositions every day. Here are some common ones:

about	by	onto
above	down	over
across	during	through
after	except	throughout
against	for	to
among	from	toward
around	in	under
at	into	up
before	near	with
beside	of	without
behind	off	
between	on	

© 2009 K12 Inc. All rights reserved.

Try It

Underline all prepositional phrases in the sentences below.
Hint: Some sentences have more than one prepositional phrase.

1. Carlo was born in New York.

2. I have a present for Dad.

3. The owl hooted during the night.

4. We'll play against your team this weekend.

5. The birds flew over our heads toward the West.

6. Everyone is going except Tom.

7. I had to sit behind my brother on the airplane.

8. I'd like to go down the Mississippi River.

9. Let's talk about the book.

10. Come stand near me under this awning, and you'll stay dry.

© 2009 K12 Inc. All rights reserved.

Sentence Completion

Choose the word from the box that best completes each sentence below. Write the word on the line provided. Then read each word aloud.

patio	poetry	radio	studio	video

1. My father wrote a book of _____ about special events in his life.

2. We could not get a clear signal on the portable _____ , so we turned it off.

3. We have lawn chairs, tables, and a grill on our _____ .

4. The _____ showed all of the customers who shopped in the store that day.

5. We went to the television _____ where they film my favorite program.

Choose two words from the box above. On the lines provided below, write a sentence that uses each word.

6. _____

_____

7. _____

_____

© 2009 K12 Inc. All rights reserved.

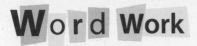
Using the Base Word *flex*

Choose a word from the box to match each definition below. Write each word in the second column.

Hint: One word will be used twice.

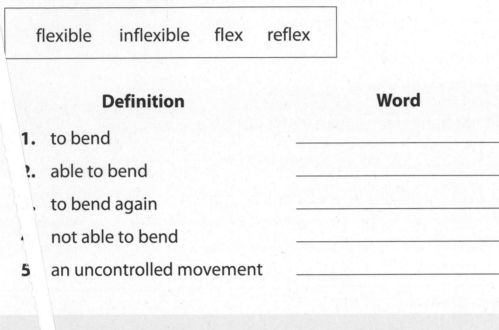

flexible   inflexible   flex   reflex

Definition	Word
1. to bend	_____
2. able to bend	_____
3. to bend again	_____
4. not able to bend	_____
5. an uncontrolled movement	_____

Choose three words from the box above. On the lines provided below, write a sentence that uses each word.

6. _____

_____

7. _____

_____

8. _____

_____

© 2009 K12 Inc. All rights reserved.

You Will Triumph

Nick turned on the radio in his bedroom. He sat at his desk and pulled out his new diary. He began to write.

January 12, 2005

Dear Diary: What a bad day. Why am I so bad at basketball? I'm tall. I'm flexible. I understand the game well. I *should* be good. Part of the problem is that my reflexes aren't great. Someone throws me the ball, and I take too long to react.

© 2009 K12 Inc. All rights reserved.

say that Paul did not help the team today. He really does need a lot more practice. But he tries hard. I know from experience--that's half the battle. Mom's calling me down for dinner. I'll write more tomorrow.

© 2009 K12 Inc. All rights reserved.

I need to work on that. It feels awful to be the last person picked each day. Jim and Nate are always the captains. They choose all the best players. That leaves me. They don't even pick me, really. I just...

© 2009 K12 Inc. All rights reserved.

feeling. "I pick Paul," I said. The gym grew silent. Ron looked at me as if I had five heads. I looked right back at him. "Paul," I said again. Paul walked over in a mix of delight and fright. "You sure about this?" he asked me. "I'm a terrible player, Nick."

"No, you're not a terrible player. You just need practice. Trust me. Stick with the sport. You have what it takes. Don't give up. You will triumph."

Paul laughed at my words. "I'm not running for president, Nick. I just want to be a good ball player."

"I know," I said, laughing. "The words sound funny now. But you'll remember them. And in a few years, you may just say th... to someone else," I have to...

© 2009 K12 Inc. All rights reserved.

end up going to the team that needs one more player. Maybe I should quit.

Nick put his diary away and turned up the radio. He tried to disappear into the music. For a moment, he forgot about the day. For the first time since he woke up, he relaxed.

"Nick! Dinner!" a voice called from downstairs. Nick jumped with a start. As he washed up for dinner, his thoughts returned to basketball. By the time he sat down, frustration was once again all over his face.

"What's the matter, son?" Nick's dad asked. "Is it basketball again?"

"Yeah," Nick said. "I'm watching videos of the best players. I'm reading about the game. I'm working hard, but I am

© 2009 K12 Inc. All rights reserved.

---

kid hasn't missed a free throw in a week. It should be a fun season. There is one boy who is not very good. His name is Paul. I see a lot of me in Paul. He is tall. He is flexible. He understands the game well. He just needs more time. I looked out on the court today as we began choosing teams. Ron, of course picked Sid first. Everyone expected me to pick Josh next. He is a super player. But I didn't. I looked out at the 15 boys holding their breath in the hopes that they would be chosen early on. And Paul had his eyes cast to the ground. It was as if he knew he would be picked last, so he didn't even bother to hope anymore. I remember that feeling. It has been four years, but I still remember that

© 2009 K12 Inc. All rights reserved.

just not getting better. And I am so tired of being picked last each day. It is a terrible feeling. I stand there and listen to every other kid's name being called. Sometimes I wish I could disappear. It's embarrassing to be chosen last every time. I wish I were as good as Jim or Nate. I think I might quit."

"You will do no such thing," Nick's dad said. "You are younger than those boys. They have had more time to improve. Give it time. Trust me. In another few years, you will be the captain. You have what it takes. Don't give up. You will triumph."

The way Nick's dad said, "You will triumph," made Nick laugh. His dad

© 2009 K12 Inc. All rights reserved.

spoke as though he were running for president or working toward world peace. But it stuck with Nick. His father had such great faith in him. He would keep practicing. Maybe someday he would be as good as Jim or Nate.

Nick turned on the radio in his bedroom. He sat as his desk and pulled out his diary. He smiled at how old and tattered it was. It held a lot of memories. He began to write.

January 5, 2009

Dear Diary: There is a lot of new talent this year. It is great because the boys have a variety of skills. Some are really fast. Some have a great jump shot. One

© 2009 K12 Inc. All rights reserved.

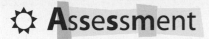 **Assessment**

Name:

Plurals & Two Vowels, Two Sounds and Base Words

Unit 6 Assessment

Part 1.

Listen to each word that is read to you. Write the words on the lines provided.

1. _____

2. _____

3. _____

4. _____

5. _____

6. _____

7. _____

8. _____

9. _____

10. _____

Part 2.

Read the singular nouns in the first column. Then write the plural form of each noun in the second column.

Singular	Plural
11. factory	
12. shelf	
13. valley	
14. hobby	
15. tomato	
16. highway	
17. discovery	
18. journey	
19. entry	
20. penny	

© 2009 K12 Inc. All rights reserved.

Part 3.

Read the plural nouns in the first column. Then write the singular form of each noun in the second column.

Plural	Singular
21. chimneys	
22. plays	
3. calves	
4. injuries	
2. wolves	
2. parties	
27. cowboys	
28. echoes	
29. families	
30. aves	

Part 4.

Listen to each word that is read to you. Write the words on the lines provided.

31. _____   36. _____

32. _____   37. _____

33. _____   38. _____

34. _____   39. _____

35. _____   40. _____

© 2009 K12 Inc. All rights reserved.

Part 5.

Read each definition below. Then underline the correct base word, root word, or suffix that matches the definition.

41. Definition: the condition of or domain

Choices: act, flex, port, struct, –ern, –dom

42. Definition: to do or to behave

Choices: act, flex, port, struct, –ern, –dom

43. Definition: to carry

Choices: act, flex, port, struct, –ern, –dom

44. Definition: to bend

Choices: act, flex, port, struct, –ern, –dom

45. Definition: to build

Choices: act, flex, port, struct, –ern, –dom

© 2009 K12 Inc. All rights reserved.

Part 6.

Each word below is missing either a base word, a root word, or a suffix. The definition tells you what the word means when the missing part is added to it. Add the correct base word, root word, or suffix to complete each word so that the words match the definitions given. An example has been done for you.

Example: star __dom__

Definition: the condition of being an outstanding performer

Choices: act, flex, port, struct, –ern, –ish, –dom

46. de _____ ive

Definition: tending toward breaking up, tearing down, ruining, or spoiling

Choices: act, flex, port, struct, –ern, –ish, –dom

47. _____ or

Definition: a person who performs in a play, on television, or in a movie

Choices: act, flex, port, struct, –ern, –ish, –dom

48. in _____ ible

Definition: not able to bend

Choices: act, flex, port, struct, –ern, –ish, –dom

49. _____ able

Definition: able to be carried

Choices: act, flex, port, struct, –ern, –ish, –dom

50. _____ ive

Definition: tending toward or full of movement

Choices: act, flex, port, struct, –ern, –ish, –dom

51. bore _____

Definition: the condition of being uninterested in something

Choices: act, flex, port, struct, –ern, –ish, –dom

© 2009 K12 Inc. All rights reserved.

Vowel Suffixes and Root Word *scrib*

Finish the Sentence

Read each of the following sentences. Complete each sentence by combining the base word and the vowel suffix listed at the end of each sentence. Write the word on the line provided. An example has been done for you.

Example: Bobby __jammed__ five cookies into his mouth. (jam, –*ed*)

1. Johnny _____ on a marble and fell down. (step, –*ed*)

2. My little brother is always _____ his drink. (spill, –*ing*)

3. Terry loves _____ cans to recycle. (smash, –*ing*)

4. My uncle _____ the flat tire on his car. (fix, –*ed*)

5. Luis _____ up all of his old toys and books. (box, –*ed*)

6. Hurry home, because Mom is _____ a good dinner. (fix, –*ing*)

7. The _____ match was very exciting to watch. (box, –*ing*)

8. Lorie _____ her orange juice all over the floor. (spill, –*ed*)

9. You are _____ too much stuff into that bag. (jam, –*ing*)

10. I like _____ in puddles when it rains. (step, –*ing*)

© 2009 K12 Inc. All rights reserved.

Root Word Crossword

Read the clues to fill in the words in the crossword below.

Hint: All of the answers use the root word *scrib*.

Across

1. to permanently print, engrave, or write on something

2. to tell all about

3. to draw or write very sloppily

Down

4. to recommend medicine

5. a person who writes

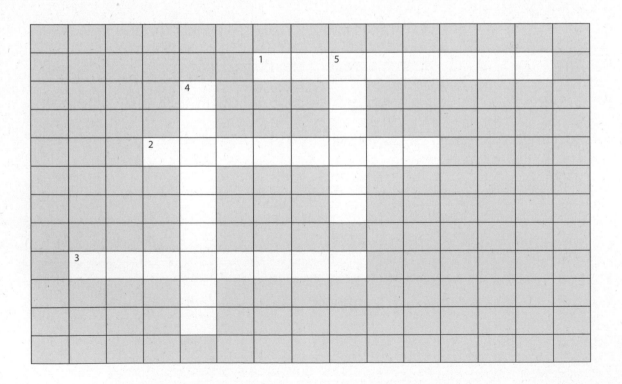

© 2009 K12 Inc. All rights reserved.

Misplacing a Dream Come True

"Thank you! Thank you! Thank you, Mom!" Reese squealed with excitement. "The Bradley Brothers are my favorite musical group! I can't believe you're giving me tickets to their next concert!" she exclaimed.

"You deserve the tickets, Reese," her mother responded. "I'm giving them to you because you've made me very proud. You study every day before you go play with your friends. You practice

© 2009 K12 Inc. All rights reserved.

"I'm not putting off the conversation, Mom. I don't need to call Tam because I found the tickets! I must have left them by the phone when I called Tam after you gave me the tickets, because there they are!" Reese exclaimed. "What a relief! I better go put these in the pocket of my jeans right now, so I don't lose them again. There's no way I'm going to miss that concert tomorrow!" Reese shouted, as she skipped to her room.

© 2009 K12 Inc. All rights reserved.

the piano without me having to ask. You keep your room clean. You always offer to help with dinner. You've become very responsible, and I'm proud of you," she said, looking at Reese with a smile. Then she gave her daughter a wink and a big hug. "So, who gets the extra ticket?" she asked.

© 2009 K12 Inc. All rights reserved.

© 2009 K12 Inc. All rights reserved.

Reese recalled. "I remember looking at the tickets as Tam and I talked about how much fun we were going to have. Oh, I forgot about Tam. I guess I should call her to tell her the bad news," Reese turned slowly and walked to the phone. How was she going to break the news to her best friend? Tam was a huge Bradley Brothers fan. She was going to be so disappointed.

As Reese reached for the phone, her expression changed. All of a sudden she was grinning from ear to ear. "There's no need for me to call Tam!" Reese told her mother.

"Reese, you can't put it off any longer. It would be impolite to wait until tomorrow to tell Tam that we aren't going to the concert."

"I'm definitely asking Tam. She's the biggest Bradley Brothers fan I know, besides me, of course!" Reese replied, as she darted off to the phone. "I'm going to call her right now to make sure she's free next Friday."

As the concert approached, Reese became more and more excited. She learned to play a Bradley Brothers song on the piano. She listened to their CD when she was cleaning her room. She hummed their songs as she helped her mother with dinner. Reese could hardly wait for the concert. Seeing the Bradley Brothers perform their music live was a dream come true. She was really looking forward to listening to their music and singing their songs with all the other fans at the concert, too.

© 2009 K12 Inc. All rights reserved.

"Well, if you didn't find them in your room, they must be somewhere else. Let's retrace your steps. What did you do with the tickets immediately after I gave them to you?" her mother asked.

"I danced around the room for a minute, and then I went to call Tam,"

© 2009 K12 Inc. All rights reserved.

On Thursday night, Reese decided to pick out what she was going to wear to the concert the next night. She opened her closet and pulled out her Bradley Brothers shirt and her favorite pair of jeans. "I'll put the concert tickets in the pocket of my jeans, so I don't forget them tomorrow," Reese said as she hung her outfit on the back of her bedroom door. She walked over to her desk to grab the tickets, but they weren't there. She checked all of the desk drawers but didn't see the tickets. "That's strange. I always keep all of my important papers on my desk or in the drawers. I'll check my bookshelf. Maybe they got stuck inside one of my books," Reese said as she continued to look around her room for the concert tickets. She searched

© 2009 K12 Inc. All rights reserved.

in her closet, under her bed, and in her nightstand, but she never found the tickets. "Oh no, this is a disaster," Reese said to herself. "Mom was so proud of me for being responsible, and now I've lost the tickets. That's the most irresponsible thing I could do!" After putting it off for almost an hour, Reese decided to tell her mother the news.

"Mom, I have some bad news," Reese said, with a look of sadness. Her mother could tell she was very upset. With a trembling voice that was barely above a whisper, Reese explained to her mother that she had lost the tickets. "I've looked all over my room and I can't find them," Reese finished.

© 2009 K12 Inc. All rights reserved.

Code **W**ork

Vowel Suffixes and Root Word *spec*

Adding Vowel Suffixes

Read the clues to fill in the words in the crossword below.

Across

1. base word *stick* + vowel suffix *–er*
5. base word *step* + vowel suffix *–ing*
7. base word *bud* + vowel suffix *–ing*
8. base word *flex* + vowel suffix *–ed*

Down

2. base word *thin* + vowel suffix *–er*
3. base word *dim* + vowel suffix *–er*
4. base word *crush* + vowel suffix *–ed*
6. base word *spill* + vowel suffix *–ed*
7. base word *blend* + vowel suffix *–er*
9. base word *fix* + vowel suffix *–ing*

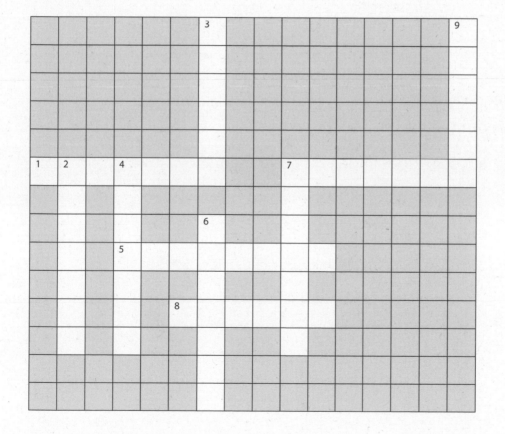

© 2009 K12 Inc. All rights reserved.

Using the Root Word *spec*

Choose a word from the box to complete each sentence below. Write each word on the line provided.

inspect	spectacles	spectator	prospect	spectacle

1. Cal was excited about the _____ of a long vacation.

2. Ben Franklin put halves of two different lenses together to make _____ that let him see both near and far.

3. Did you _____ the vase carefully to make sure it was not broken?

4. The reporter picked one _____ to interview about the exciting hockey game.

5. The performance included fireworks and a light show. It was quite a _____ !

Choose a word from the box above. On the lines provided below, write a sentence that uses that word.

6. _____

_____

© 2009 K12 Inc. All rights reserved.

Get Ready

🔲 *Between* and *among* are prepositions that people often confuse.

🔲 Use *between* when you are discussing **two** people, places, things, or ideas, or **two groups** of people, places, things, or ideas. For example:

> There are six houses and ten trees *between* you and me.
>
> Please put the rubies *between* the sapphires and emeralds.

🔲 Use *among* when you are discussing **more than two** people, places, things, or ideas, or **more than two groups**. For example:

> *Among* all her friends, Jim is the most reliable.
>
> Bill had a hard time choosing *among* all the college courses.

🔲 *From* and *off* are also prepositions that people sometimes misuse. Both relate to distance or separation, but these prepositions aren't synonyms.

🔲 *From* can show the source of something.

> We buy corn *from* the farmers' market.

🔲 *From* can also show distance in time or space.

> The farmers' market is three miles *from* here.

🔲 *Off*, when used as a preposition, can mean "down from" or "away from."

> The acrobat fell *off* the tightrope.

🔲 Notice: It is incorrect to use the phrase "off of." "The acrobat fell *off the* tightrope" is correct. Avoid writing "the acrobat fell *off of the* tightrope."

© 2009 K12 Inc. All rights reserved.

Try It

In each sentence below, underline the correct preposition in parentheses that completes the sentence.

1. Careful! Don't fall (off of, off) that ladder.

2. When you sit at the table, take (from, off) your hat.

3. Jenny walked (among, between) her three sisters.

4. It was hard to get the lid (off of, off) the jam.

5. You may sit (between, among) Mom and me.

6. Take the phone message (from, off) Bob, please.

7. The two girls carried the trunk (among, between) them.

8. No one (among, between) the campers raised their hand.

On the lines provided below, write sentences that use each of the prepositions given.

9. among _____

_____

10. between _____

_____

11. from _____

_____

12. off _____

_____

© 2009 K12 Inc. All rights reserved.

Vowel Suffixes

Add the suffix in the Suffix column to the base word in the Base Word column. Then draw a ✓ in the column telling what you must do to the base word before adding that suffix. Write the new word in the New Word column. The first one has been done for you.

Base Word	Suffix	Make No Change	Double the Final Letter	Drop the *e*	New Word
humiliate	–ing			✓	humiliating
race	–ed				
step	–ing				
starve	–ation				
wish	–ed				
clap	–ed				
hope	–ing				
motivate	–ion				
stop	–ed				
kick	–ing				

© 2009 K12 Inc. All rights reserved.

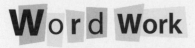

Vowel Suffixes and Root Word *val*

A *Val*uable Word Search

The root *val* means "worth." All of the words below are related because they contain the root *val*. Each word in the box appears in the word search chart below. Find and circle each word in the chart. Words may appear across, down, or backward.

value	valuable	evaluate	valiant
valor	valueless	valid	

v	a	n	w	l	o	n	a	o	l
	e	v	a	l	u	a	t	e	n
	v	a	l	u	e	l	e	s	s
u	l	l	t	p	d	d	b	w	i
a	t	o	f	b	a	i	l	l	e
b	r	t	w	e	l	o	p	u	
l	n	e	y	u	a	k	n	l	
e	s	a	o	m	a	v	e	b	a
l	e	p	t	n	a	i	l	a	v
u	t	u	l	s	n	r	p	d	e

© 2009 K12 Inc. All rights reserved.

A Garden of Surprises

"Grandma, I love your garden. It's one of my favorite things about visiting you. The flowers are so pretty and they smell great. Hummingbirds and butterflies seem to agree with me, because they are always fluttering around. I could spend all day watching them dance from flower to flower," Chen said to his grandmother, as they sat in her backyard.

© 2009 K12 Inc. All rights reserved.

© 2009 K12 Inc. All rights reserved.

"I knew you'd be impressed," his grandmother smiled. "There's only one more thing we need to do," she said. Chen looked confused. "We need to stop calling it my garden, because now it's our garden," his grandmother explained. Then they spent the rest of the day watching the hummingbirds and butterflies dance from flower to flower.

His grandmother smiled. "Would you like me to teach you about the different flowers in my garden?" she asked. "Maybe one day you'll be able to use what I teach you and plant a garden of your own."

"I'd love that," Chen replied. His grandmother led him around her garden. As they walked, she named each flower and told him everything she knew about it. By the time she finished, Chen had a better understanding of how to plant and care for a garden.

"I may not be ready to plant my own garden, but I hope you'll let me help you take care of yours when I visit," Chen said. "I'll be back again next month. Do you think I can help you then?"

© 2009 K12 Inc. All rights reserved.

When she opened the door, Chen's expression changed. His eyes grew huge, and a smile covered his face.

"Look at your garden!" Chen shouted. "It's more beautiful than I've ever seen it!"

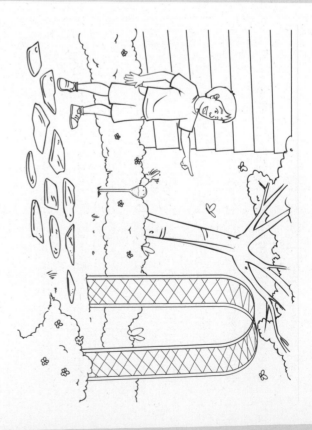

© 2009 K12 Inc. All rights reserved.

"I would love your help, Chen. There will be plenty to do when you come back," she assured.

The weeks flew by for Chen, and before he knew it, it was time to visit his grandmother again. He was excited to spend time with her, and to try his hand at gardening. When he arrived at his grandmother's house, he gave her a big hug and immediately went to see her garden. As soon as he stepped outside, he froze. Chen couldn't believe his eyes.

"Grandma, what happened to your garden? Where are all the flowers?" he asked.

"I had to trim them back. This is the time of year when we prepare the flowers for the next blooming season,"

© 2009 K12 Inc. All rights reserved.

Chen's grandmother could tell Chen was still uncertain. Yet she knew that he would understand soon enough. She spent the rest of the day teaching Chen how to prepare the soil and plant seeds and bulbs. When they were finished, Chen looked around. He was unable to hide the look of sadness on his face.

"I know the garden looks different now than it did a month ago, but soon you'll see that the changes were worth it," his grandmother predicted.

Several months later, Chen made another trip to his grandmother's house. He was happy to see her, but he wasn't as excited about her garden as he had been in the past. When he arrived, his grandmother gave him a big hug and immediately led him to the backyard.

© 2009 K12 Inc. All rights reserved.

his grandmother explained. "It might not look as pretty as you remembered it, but with the right care, it will be even more beautiful in a few months. Are you ready to help me?" she asked.

© 2009 K12 Inc. All rights reserved.

© 2009 K12 Inc. All rights reserved.

"What do you mean? It doesn't look like there's anything for me to help you do. Most of the flowers are gone. The ones that are left are cut pretty short," Chen replied.

His grandmother could tell that Chen was disappointed. She looked at him and smiled. "What you don't understand, Chen, is that this is when I need your help more than ever. We have to pull weeds and prepare the soil. Then we need to plant seeds and bulbs. This is how a beautiful garden begins," she said. She grabbed a pair of gloves and some gardening tools and handed them to Chen. "Do you still want to help?"

"Of course I do," he answered. "If this is how you make your garden beautiful, I want to help."

Name:

Vowel Suffixes

Add a vowel suffix to each word below as indicated. The first one has been done for you.

1. base word *balance* + vowel suffix *–ed*   balanced

2. base word *starve* + vowel suffix *–ation*   _____

3. base word *share* + vowel suffix *–ing*   _____

4. base word *locate* + vowel suffix *–ion*   _____

5. base word *relieve* + vowel suffix *–ed*   _____

6. base word *excite* + vowel suffix *–ing*   _____

Choose the word formed above that best completes each sentence below. Write the words on the lines provided.

7. Without any food to eat, the animals were in danger of

    _____ .

8. We followed the treasure map to find the _____ of the gold.

9. I always pack extra food for lunch, because I enjoy

    _____ with others.

10. Jane was _____ to find out that she had no cavities.

11. The performer _____ a spinning bowl on his head.

12. It is an _____ day for Chad; he is getting a new puppy!

© 2009 K12 Inc. All rights reserved.

The Root Word *rupt*

All of the words below contain the root *rupt*. Read each word and its definition. Then choose the word that best completes each sentence below. Write that word on the line provided.

Word	Meaning
rupture	to break or tear apart
interrupt	to stop by breaking in, as one would interrupt a conversation
disrupt	to disturb or interrupt the process of an activity
erupt	to break out or burst forth suddenly and violently
corrupt	to change from the correct version of something to a damaged version

1. Please do not _____ me when I am on the telephone.

2. Scientists think that the volcano is ready to _____ .

3. This file is _____ ; it was damaged when my computer crashed.

4. If you _____ a heart muscle, Dr. Jonas is the man to see—he is a heart specialist.

5. If you continue to _____ my concentration, it will take me forever to finish my homework.

© 2009 K12 Inc. All rights reserved.

Get Ready

▪ An *adverbial phrase* is a prepositional phrase used as an adverb. The phrase tells more about the verb. An adverbial phrase contains a preposition and an object.

▪ Look at these sentences with adverbial phrases. The verbs (in bold) are described by the underlined adverbial phrase.

The frightened cat **scrambled** up the oak tree.

From the empty room **came** strange noises.

He **looked** inside the drawer but couldn't find the missing sock.

▪ Notice the position of each adverbial phrase—an adverbial phrase can appear anywhere in the sentence. Notice also that each adverbial phrase has a preposition and an object.

Adverbial Phrase	Preposition	Object
…up the oak tree.	up	the oak tree
From the empty room…	From	the empty room
…inside the drawer	inside	the drawer

© 2009 K12 Inc. All rights reserved.

Try It

Complete each sentence with an adverbial phrase. Write each phrase on the line provided.

1. The bird flies _____.

2. We traveled _____.

3. Dad reached _____.

4. Jill ate _____.

5. I put the books _____.

6. The cat ran _____.

7. Alan bought _____.

8. After dinner, we went _____.

© 2009 K12 Inc. All rights reserved.

Vowel Suffix Practice

Add the suffix in the Suffix column to the base word in the Base Word column. Draw a ✓ in the column that tells what you must do to the base word before adding that suffix. Write the new word in the final column. The first one has been done for you.

Hint: If the accent or stress in the word is on the second syllable, double the last consonant before adding the suffix.

Base Word	Suffix	Double the Final Letter and Add the Suffix	Just Add the Suffix	Base Word with Suffix
1. refer	–ing	✓		referring
2. matter	–ed			
3. offer	–ed			
4. rebel	–ed			
5. cover	–ing			
6. shelter	–ed			
7. propel	–ing			
8. anger	–ed			
9. occur	–ing			
10. suffer	–ing			
11. defer	–ing			
12. label	–ed			
13. gather	–ing			
14. prefer	–ed			

© 2009 K12 Inc. All rights reserved.

Using the Root *dict*

The root *dict* means "to say or inform." Choose a word from the box to match each phrase below. Write each word on the line provided.
Hint: One word will be used twice.

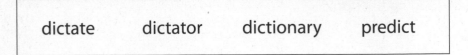

dictate   dictator   dictionary   predict

1. a ruler with power over a country _____

2. to speak or read something aloud for someone to write down

   _____

3. to say what one believes will happen in the future _____

4. a book of information about words _____

5. to order or command _____

On the lines provided below, write sentences that use each word from the box above.

6. _____

   _____

7. _____

   _____

8. _____

   _____

9. _____

   _____

© 2009 K12 Inc. All rights reserved.

Improving with Practice

Kim stood backstage with her best friend Lynn. They peeked out through the curtains to look at the crowd. "Look at all those people," Lynn said. "I'm nervous."

"Why are you nervous?" Kim asked. "You've been performing at piano recitals for years. You should be used to big crowds by now."

© 2009 K12 Inc. All rights reserved.

"That's great news, Kim. I knew you could do it," Lynn said. "Maybe we could play a duet at the next recital," she offered.

"That sounds fun," Kim replied. "I'll have to practice extra hard to keep up with you. I know now that even though it looks easy, playing the piano takes practice." The girls spent the rest of the phone call deciding on the song they wanted to learn for the recital. Kim knew it would be difficult in the beginning, but she knew that with patience and hard work, she could learn the song and make it look easy.

© 2009 K12 Inc. All rights reserved.

"This may not be my first recital, but I still get nervous," Lynn said. "I'm excited, too. I've been practicing for months. I'm ready for everyone to hear me play."

Kim wished Lynn good luck. Then she left Lynn to take a seat with Lynn's family. After a few minutes, the lights dimmed and the curtains opened.

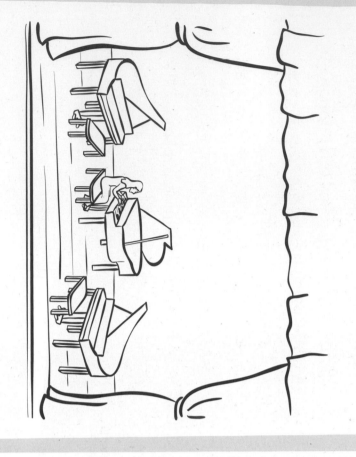

© 2009 K12 Inc. All rights reserved.

---

songs before you know it," Lynn assured Kim.

Kim continued her piano lessons. She eventually mastered scales. Then she was able to move on to her first song. It took several lessons, but she learned how to play the song all the way through without making any mistakes. Without her realizing it, playing the piano had become easier for Kim. She called Lynn to tell her the good news.

"You were right, Lynn," Kim began. "Playing the piano was tough in the beginning, but it's getting easier. I'm really enjoying learning to play new music. It's challenging, but it's very rewarding!"

© 2009 K12 Inc. All rights reserved.

The group performances were first.

Then it was on to solos. Lynn was the final solo performer. Kim was amazed by how calm Lynn looked. No one would ever know she had told Kim backstage that she was nervous. Lynn performed her solo flawlessly.

On the way home, Kim told Lynn she wanted to play the piano, too. Lynn thought that was a great idea. She encouraged Kim to take lessons with her teacher.

A week later, Kim was sitting on a piano bench next to Lynn's piano teacher. This was her first lesson, but she was already imagining herself playing

© 2009 K12 Inc. All rights reserved.

"It was so boring," Kim complained. "I didn't play any music. I just played scales."

"I know it seems boring now, but scales are important. Were you able to learn the notes quickly?" Lynn asked.

"That's the other problem. The teacher made the scales seem so easy, but my fingers just couldn't seem to touch the right keys," Kim responded.

"I thought playing the piano was going to be easy. You make it look so effortless."

"Don't forget, Kim, I've been playing the piano for years. Even though it's easier for me now, I started out just like you. I still have a little trouble when I learn new songs. It takes practice, but it's worth it. Trust me, you'll be

© 2009 K12 Inc. All rights reserved.

© 2009 K12 Inc. All rights reserved.

the same songs that Lynn played at her recital. Kim was disappointed when the teacher began the lesson by explaining the parts of a piano. After hearing about the piano keys and foot pedals,

© 2009 K12 Inc. All rights reserved.

Kim thought that she would finally be able to start playing a song. Her piano teacher had other plans. She started teaching Kim how to play scales.

The teacher explained that scales are a group of notes played in order. "By learning to play scales," she said, "you'll be able to play more difficult music later." Even though scales sounded easy when the teacher played them, Kim quickly realized that they were harder than she thought.

Kim called Lynn as soon as she got home from her first lesson. "Hi, Kim. How was your first piano lesson?" Lynn asked.

Name: _____

Vowel Suffixes and Root Word *tract*

Vowel Suffix Practice

Add the suffix in the Suffix column to each base word in the Base Word column below. Next, put a ✓ in the column that tells what you must do to the base word when you add a vowel suffix. Then write the word with the suffix in the Base Word with Suffix column.

Hint: If the accent or stress is on the second syllable, double the last consonant before adding the suffix.

Base Word	Suffix	Double the Final Letter and Add the Suffix	Just Add the Suffix	Base Word with Suffix
shatter	–ing			
whisper	–ed			
transfer	–ed			
order	–ed			
commit	–ing			
honor	–ed			
submit	–ed			
equip	–ed			
regret	–ed			
flutter	–ing			

© 2009 K12 Inc. All rights reserved.

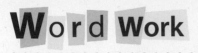

Vowel Suffixes and Root Word *tract*

Using the Root *tract*

The root *tract* means "to pull or to drag." Choose a word from the box to match each phrase below. Write each word on the line provided.

| distract | subtract | traction | tractor |

1. a powerful vehicle used for pulling farm machinery   _____

2. the power to grip or hold to a surface when moving   _____

3. to pull away or to take a smaller number from a larger number   _____

4. to pull someone's attention away from someone or something   _____

On the lines provided below, write sentences that use three of the words from the box above.

5. _____

_____

6. _____

_____

7. _____

_____

© 2009 K12 Inc. All rights reserved.

Suffix Scramble

Add suffix in Suffix column to each base word in Base Word column. Next, put a ✓ in the column that tells what you must do to that base word when adding that suffix. Write each base word with suffix added in the Base Word with Suffix column. The first one has been done for you.

Base Word	Suffix	Change the *y* to *i*	Keep the *y*	Base Word with Suffix
relay	–ing		✓	relaying
heavy				
betray				
_____				
tiny				
lazy				
survey				
display				
cozy				
chunky				
portray				
silly				
imply				

© 2009 K12 Inc. All rights reserved.

Name:

Vowel Suffixes and Root Word *fer*

The Root *fer*

Draw a line from each word with the root *fer* to its definition.

1. ferry   a meeting of people brought together to discuss something

2. conference   to move, carry, send, or change from one person or place to another

3. prefer   to present to be accepted or rejected

4. transfer   a boat used for taking people or cars across water

5. offer   to send to a person or place for treatment, help, advice, or information

6. refer   to like better

Choose the word from above that best completes each sentence below. Write that word on the line provided.

7. My mom will _____ the hot dish from the oven to the table.

8. I _____ to exercise in the morning.

9. Many world leaders will attend the _____ in India.

10. We took a _____ to the island.

11. I will _____ you to a good doctor.

12. I know my sister will _____ to give me a ride to the mall.

© 2009 K12 Inc. All rights reserved.

A New Perspective

Will and Zach were brothers. They were also best friends. They listened to the same kind of music. They played the same sports. They read the same magazines. They spent much of their free time together. Will and Zach were very close. Will was three years older than Zach. This fall, Will was starting college in a nearby city. Zach was happy and excited for his brother. He was also

© 2009 K12 Inc. All rights reserved.

---

see me. It won't be the same as walking down the hall or driving a few minutes to get to your college, but it will help make the distance seem smaller."

Will looked at his brother and smiled. He thanked him for apologizing. Then they spent the rest of the afternoon talking about the fun and exciting things in Will's future.

© 2009 K12 Inc. All rights reserved.

looking forward to visiting his brother on campus. Zach's plans were turned upside down when Will came to him with an announcement.

"Zach, I want to talk to you about me starting college," Will began.

"I can't wait! I want to hear all about your interesting classes. I want to meet your new friends. I'm really looking forward to you showing me around campus. I'll drive to come see you any chance I get," Zach rattled.

"That's what I want to talk to you about, Zach. Remember how I applied to two colleges?" Will asked.

"Yes, and I'm so glad you chose the one closest to home. The other college was so far away. We would only have

© 2009 K12 Inc. All rights reserved.

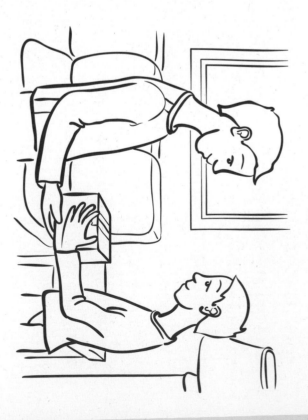

"You'll see when you open it," Zach replied. Will unwrapped the package and found a small camera. "It's a webcam," Zach explained. "You put it on your computer, and I can see you when we talk over the Internet. I bought one for our computer here, too, so you can

© 2009 K12 Inc. All rights reserved.

seen each other when you came home during school breaks," Zach replied.

"You seem to have forgotten that I chose the closer college because I never heard back from the other one," Will reminded.

"It doesn't matter why you're going to the closer one. It only matters that you'll be within driving distance," Zach said.

"Well, I received a letter from the second college. The letter said that they have accepted me. I've thought about it, and I've decided to go there instead," Will explained. He could see the disappointment on Zach's face.

"This changes everything," Zach said. "I'm not going to know what's going on in your life. We'll only see each other every couple of months."

© 2009 K12 Inc. All rights reserved.

---

he was behaving. He was looking at the situation only from his perspective. Of course he was going to miss Will. Of course things would be different without Will living in the same house, or even in a nearby city. That didn't mean that he shouldn't be happy for his brother. Will was beginning a new and exciting chapter in his life, but he couldn't share his excitement with his best friend. At that moment, Zach made a decision.

The next day, Zach talked to Will. He apologized for being selfish and making it hard for Will to be excited. Then he handed Will a small package. "What's this?" Will asked.

© 2009 K12 Inc. All rights reserved.

© 2009 K12 Inc. All rights reserved.

4

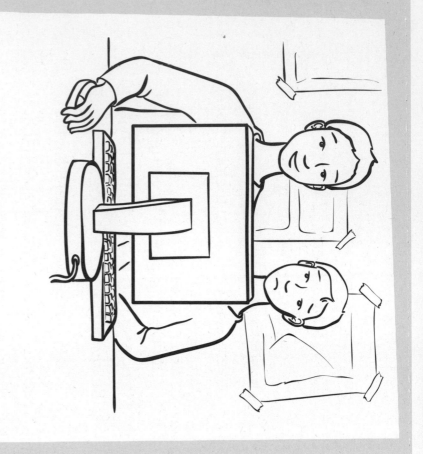

"I know things will be different, Zach, but it won't be so bad. We'll still talk on the phone. We can write letters and e-mail. We'll still keep in touch," Will assured him, though Zach didn't seem convinced.

© 2009 K12 Inc. All rights reserved.

5

Will spent the next few weeks talking about the campus and the classes he wanted to take. He and Zach looked at the college's website together. They read articles written by students describing life on campus. During this time, Zach couldn't help thinking about how different life was going to be. How boring life would be without his brother. His brother was going to have a whole new life that didn't include Zach.

One day, Zach overheard Will talking to their parents. He was telling them that he was sad that Zach was taking the news so hard. Will wanted to be excited about leaving, but he couldn't when he knew that Zach was so unhappy. At that moment, Zach realized how selfishly

Suffix Scramble

Read the base word and suffix in each row of the chart below. Draw a ✓ in the column that correctly states what you must do to each base word when you add that suffix. In the Base Word with Suffix column, write the new word with the suffix added. The first one is done for you.

Base Word	Suffix	Change the y to i	Keep the y	Base Word with Suffix
betray	–ed		✓	betrayed
survey	–ed			
relay	–ing			
heavy	–er			
tiny	–est			

Choose the new word from above that best completes each sentence below. Write each word on the line provided.

1. My suitcase is _____ than yours.

2. The farmer _____ his field of wheat before harvesting it.

3. Mary _____ her friend by telling her friend's secret.

4. The ship's captain received a distress message and began _____ it to other ships in the area.

5. We chose the _____ kitten from the litter of six.

© 2009 K12 Inc. All rights reserved.

Name:

The Root *vis*

Draw a line from each word with the root *vis* to its definition.

1. visitor   the act or power of seeing

2. vision   not able to be seen or noticed

3. invisible   a distant view of natural beauty

4. vista   able to be seen or noticed

5. visible   one who visits or comes to be seen

Choose the word from above that best completes each sentence below.
Write that word on the line provided.

6. The stain on my shirt is so light that it's almost _____ .

7. We stopped at a beautiful _____ to take a picture of the view.

8. Some organisms are so small that they are not

   _____ to the human eye.

9. Jane was surprised to hear her doorbell because she rarely

   gets a _____ .

10. When I had trouble with my _____ , I went to an eye doctor.

© 2009 K12 Inc. All rights reserved.

Get Ready

- A *phrase* is a group of related words. *Prepositional phrases* do the job of a single modifier. Prepositions include *at*, *by*, *for*, *from*, *in*, *on*, *to*, and *with*.

- *Adverbial phrases* are prepositional phrases that take the place of an adverb. The adverbial phrase modifies a verb, an adjective, or an adverb.

> The boys ran *into the gym*.

- *Adjectival phrases* are prepositional phrases that take the place of an adjective. The adjectival phrase modifies a noun or pronoun. In the sentences below, the adjectival phrase is in italics, and the noun or pronoun that it modifies is in bold.

> The **boys** *with the blue shirts* ran.
>
> The **girls** *in the wagon* giggled.
>
> The **dog** *near the fence* was barking.
>
> The **lamp** *on the table* fell over.
>
> **Everybody** *except you* is going.

- Notice that the adjectival phrase comes right after the noun or pronoun that the phrase modifies.

© 2009 K12 Inc. All rights reserved.

Try It

Read the sentences below. Circle the adjectival phrase in each sentence. On each line provided, write the noun that is modified by that adjectival phrase.

1. The flowers in the vase smell beautiful. _____

2. They are from the garden around back. _____

3. The tulips beside the fence are pink, purple, and red. _____

4. The lilacs by the oak tree are getting big. _____

I love to plant flowers with lots of colors. _____

We also planted tomato plants from the market. _____

I love to eat tomatoes with cheese and basil. _____

8. Next year, I will plant some basil for my kitchen. _____

© 2009 K12 Inc. All rights reserved.

Name:

Vowel Suffixes and Root Word *cur*

Complete the Sentence

Complete each sentence by combining the base word and vowel suffix given in parentheses. Write the new word on the line provided. The first one has been done for you.

1. The __batter__ swung at the ball and hit a home run!
   (bat, –*er*)

2. We _____ the cans before we tossed them in the bir
   (crush, –*ed*)

3. The balloon _____ floated away.
   (float, –*ed*)

4. My mother _____ the lights during the movie
   (dim, –*ed*)

5. Mel enjoys _____ her hair.
   (braid, –*ing*)

6. My father is washing and _____ ou ar this weekend.
   (wax, –*ing*)

7. I _____ the plate before it fell onto the floor.
   (grab, –*ed*)

8. Shawn _____ his foot while he played his saxophone.
   (tap, –*ed*)

9. He used a _____ to combine the ingredients for the cake.
   (mix, –*er*)

10. We were _____ in line to pay for our purchases
    (wait, –*ing*)

© 2009 K12 Inc. All rights reserved.

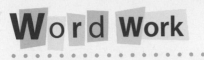

Name:

Vowel Suffixes and Root Word *cur*

Using the Root *cur*

Choose a word from the box to match each definition below. Write the word on the line provided. Read aloud each word that you write.

Hint: One word will be used twice.

current	cursive	currency	concur

1. flowing writing with joined letters _____

2. to act together or to approve; to agree with _____

3. the flow of water, air, or electricity _____

4. money in actual use in a country _____

5. now going on _____

Choose three words from the box above. Write a sentence that uses each word on the lines provided below.

6. _____

_____

7. _____

_____

8. _____

_____

© 2009 K12 Inc. All rights reserved.

"Dad, I've had a weird feeling all day. I think people have been watching me. Even worse, I'm pretty sure people have been taking pictures and filming me," Rose said.

"I'm glad you came to me, Rose. How about if you don't walk to practice or ride your bike to volunteer tomorrow? I'll drive you, instead. That way, if someone is following you, I'll know," her father suggested.

Rose felt a little more comfortable. However, she thought it was odd that her father didn't seem more concerned. As soon as they arrived home, her father jumped out of the car. "Let's head inside."

© 2009 K12 Inc. All rights reserved.

explained that the manager at the animal shelter nominated Rose to be the focus of a news segment. The manager was proud of Rose. She thought Rose was a good example of how teenagers can balance their time between fun activities and helping others.

Rose felt proud. She was also surprised. She had no idea that other people thought so highly of her. She turned to her father. "When did you find out about this?" Rose asked.

"The manager at the animal shelter called me last week. That's when she told me her plan. She's very proud of you, and she's not the only one. When

© 2009 K12 Inc. All rights reserved.

The local news starts in a few minutes. I'd like to catch it at the beginning," he explained.

"Maybe he is more worried than he's letting show," Rose said to herself. "Maybe he wants to watch the news to see if there have been any reports of strange people around town."

Rose sat with her father on the couch. They watched as reporters updated them on the local news. Suddenly, one of the reporters caught Rose's eye. "That's him! That's the person who was talking to Coach Woods during practice! I knew I wasn't going crazy! Dad, that's one of the people I caught watching me today," Rose exclaimed. She turned to look at

© 2009 K12 Inc. All rights reserved.

her father. Rose was confused when she saw him smiling. "Why are you smiling, Dad? This is serious. That reporter was following me today," Rose said.

"Rose, I think if you watch the news for a few more minutes, you'll see why I'm smiling," her father explained. At that moment, Rose heard the reporter say her name. He described how Rose is helpful at home. How she participates in local clubs, yet she still finds time to volunteer at the local animal shelter. The report showed pictures of Rose raking leaves. It included quotes from her soccer coach. There was also video footage of Rose at the animal shelter. Suddenly, it all made sense. Rose began to smile. She continued to listen to the reporter. He

© 2009 K12 Inc. All rights reserved.

Adding Vowel Suffixes

Read the clues to form the words that fill in the crossword below.

Across

1. base word *enjoy* + vowel suffix –*ed*

2. base word *bake* + vowel suffix –*ing*

5. base word *lucky* + vowel suffix –*est*

6. base word *employ* + vowel suffix –*ed*

7. base word *calculate* + vowel suffix –*ing*

9. base word *care* + vowel suffix –*ing*

Down

3. base word *poke* + vowel suffix –*ed*

4. base word *grumpy* + vowel suffix –*er*

8. base word *excuse* + vowel suffix –*ed*

10. base word *funny* + vowel suffix –*er*

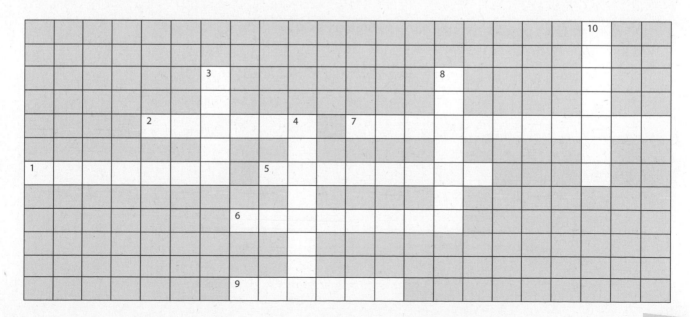

© 2009 K12 Inc. All rights reserved.

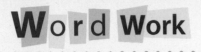
Using the Root *ven*

The root *ven* means "to come." Choose a word from the box to match each phrase below. Write each word on the line provided.

| convene | convention | intervene | invent |

1. to come between or interrupt people or events _____

2. to create or come up with, through thought or imagination _____

3. a formal meeting where people come to discuss something in common _____

4. to assemble or to come together _____

On the first lines provided below, write a definition for the word *prevent*. Make sure to use the meaning of the root *ven* in your definition. Then write a sentence that uses the word *prevent* on the next lines provided.

prevent

Definition: _____

_____

Sentence: _____

_____

© 2009 K12 Inc. All rights reserved.

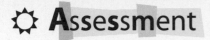
Unit 7 Assessment

Part 1.

Listen to each word that is read to you. Write the words on the lines provided.

1. _____   6. _____

2. _____   7. _____

3. _____   8. _____

4. _____   9. _____

5. _____   10. _____

Part 2.

Combine the base word and vowel suffix that are listed to make a new word. Write the words on the lines provided. An example has been done for you.

Example: (jam, –*ed*)   _jammed_____

11. (order, –*ed*)   _____

12. (regret, –*ing*)   _____

13. (employ, –*ed*)   _____

14. (supply, –*ing*)   _____

15. (grumpy, –*er*)   _____

16. (excuse, –*ing*)   _____

17. (fix, –*ed*)   _____

© 2009 K12 Inc. All rights reserved.

Part 3.

Read the sentences below. Underline *true* if the spelling rule is correct; underline *false* if the spelling rule is incorrect.

18. When a one-syllable word ends in two or more consonants, the base word keeps its original spelling when a vowel suffix is added. (true, false)

19. When a one-syllable word ends with the letter *x*, the *x* is doubled before a vowel suffix is added. (true, false)

20. When a base word ends in silent *e*, the base word keeps its original spelling when a vowel suffix is added. (true, false)

21. When the second syllable of a two-syllable word is stressed, the last consonant of the base word is doubled before a vowel suffix is added. (true, false)

© 2009 K12 Inc. All rights reserved.

Vowel Suffixes and Root Words

Part 4.

Read each definition below. Then select the correct root or base word from the box that matches each definition, and write that word on the line provided.

cur	fer	script	tract	ven
dict	rupt	spec	val	vis

22. Definition: to write

Answer: _____

23. Definition: to look or to watch

Answer: _____

24. Definition: worth

Answer: _____

25. Definition: to break

Answer: _____

26. Definition: to say or to inform

Answer: _____

27. Definition: to pull or to drag

Answer: _____

28. Definition: to carry or to bring

Answer: _____

29. Definition: to see

Answer: _____

30. Definition: to run or to flow

Answer: _____

31. Definition: to come

Answer: _____

© 2009 K12 Inc. All rights reserved.

Part 5.

Choose the word from the box that best completes each sentence below.
Write that word on the line provided.

prescription	dictionary	scribbles	prefer
tractor	cursive	invisible	inspects
convention	interrupts	valuable	

32. The tires on the _____ are taller than my father.

33. I _____ riding my bike over walking.

34. My _____ writing is a little messy because I am still learning.

35. The doctor wrote a _____ for some medicine.

36. My little brother cannot write the alphabet, so he just

_____ .

37. My aunt's antique table is very _____ .

38. I used the _____ to learn how to pronounce that word.

39. I think it would be fun to be _____ for a day and to play tricks on my sister!

40. My father always _____ fruits and vegetables carefully before he buys them.

41. Chandra gets upset when her brother _____ her while she is talking.

42. Artists from all around the country traveled to the

_____ .

© 2009 K12 Inc. All rights reserved.

Contraction Concentration

Complete the sentences below by writing the letters on the lines provided.

1. When a contraction is formed that uses the word *not*, an apostrophe replaces the letter _____.

2. When a contraction is formed that uses the word *have*, an apostrophe replaces the letters _____ and _____ .

Use the two words in the first column to form a contraction in the second column. The first one has been done for you.

should have	should've
they have	
did not	
could have	
will not	
should not	
cannot	
does not	
you have	
has not	
would have	
I have	

© 2009 K12 Inc. All rights reserved.

The Root *cap*

The root *cap* means "to take." Review the following definitions of four words that contain the root *cap*. Then complete each sentence below by using one of the words. Write each word on the line provided.

Word	Meaning
capture	to catch and hold by force or skill
captivate	to take someone's interest
captor	someone who takes a prisoner captive
captive	to be held or taken prisoner

1. The little lost dog seemed to _____ everyone, and several people offered to take it home.

2. The prisoner tried to escape from his _____ by hiding in the forest.

3. We played a game this afternoon where Samantha was a pirate who took us _____ .

4. When my pet mouse got out of its cage, it took two days for us to finally find and _____ it.

© 2009 K12 Inc. All rights reserved.

Get Ready

■ A *conjunction* is a word that joins words or groups of words. Three of the most common conjunctions are *and*, *but*, and *or*.

■ *And*, *but*, and *or* have very different meanings. The examples below will show you how to use the right conjunction to say what you want to say.

> *And* joins ideas that are similar or equal.
> He *and* Paul are best friends.

> *But* joins ideas that are different or show contrast.
> Bill can skateboard, *but* he can't skate.

> *Or* joins ideas that give a choice or an alternative.
> I can't decide whether to get a cat *or* a dog.

■ If a sentence has more than one subject, that sentence has a compound subject. Conjunctions usually join the subjects. In the examples below, the subjects are in bold and the conjunction is in italics.

> **He** *and* **Paul** are best friends.

> **Skateboarding** *but* not **skating** is what Bill likes.

> **Dogs** *or* **cats** are common family pets.

© 2009 K12 Inc. All rights reserved.

Try It

Read each sentence below. Fill in the line provided with a conjunction. Circle the subjects that each conjunction connects.

1. Jake _____ I like to ride bikes. We ride everyday.

2. Not Marissa _____ Alexis will meet us at the park on Sunday.

3. I like making jumps to ride over. Not Mom _____ Dad helps me make the jumps.

4. Dad _____ Mom helps me put on my helmet and pads.

5. Jake _____ Alexis will practice riding on Saturday.

© 2009 K12 Inc. All rights reserved.

"Addition" with Contractions

Complete the sentences below by writing the correct letter or letters on the lines provided.

1. When you form a contraction using the word *not*, an apostrophe replaces the letter _____ .

2. When you form a contraction using the word *have*, an apostrophe replaces the letters _____ and _____ .

3. When you form a contraction using the word *will*, an apostrophe replaces the letters _____ and _____ .

4. When you form a contraction using the word *is*, an apostrophe replaces the letter _____ .

Fill in the blank lines below. The first one has been done for you.
Hint: Watch out for number 12. It does not follow the rules above.

5. they + will = they'll

6. what + is = _____

7. _____ + will = she'll

8. could + not = _____

9. you + have = _____

10. that + is = _____

11. I + will = _____

12. will + not = _____

13. it + _____ = it's

14. _____ + will = you'll

15. he + is = _____

© 2009 K12 Inc. All rights reserved.

The Root *cred*

The root *cred* means "to believe." Review the following definitions, and then use each of the words that are defined below to complete the sentences. Write the words on the lines provided.

Word	Meaning
credible	worthy of belief; believable
incredible	very great, unusual, or special in a way that makes it hard or impossible to believe
credit	belief or trust, or praise or approval
discredit	to spoil the good reputation of another or to create doubts about someone or something
credence	an acceptance of something as real or true
credential	creating confidence or credit

1. The most _____ thing happened yesterday. I could tell you about it, but you probably wouldn't believe me.

2. We thought it was just a rumor, but Mr. Jacobs gave

   _____ to it, and now we believe that it's true.

3. Her nursing _____ enables her to work in any hospital in the country.

4. I will find proof to _____ what you say. I know Victor is innocent.

5. I give you _____ for telling the truth, even though you knew you would get in trouble for lying.

6. Though it sounds almost impossible, Jack's story is

   _____ . I know because I was there.

© 2009 K12 Inc. All rights reserved.

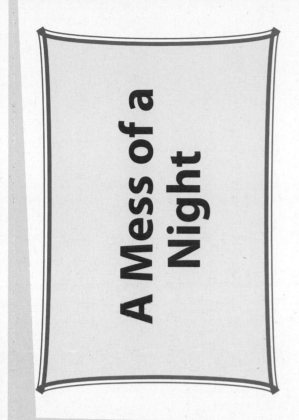

A Mess of a Night

I just survived the hardest day of my life. Well, maybe it wasn't the hardest day of my life, but it certainly felt like it. It probably didn't help that I wasn't prepared. I didn't have a plan, because I thought things would be easy. Boy, was I wrong! Taking care of my little sister was so much harder than I expected!

It all started when my parents received an invitation to a dinner party. I thought it would be nice to help out,

© 2009 K12 Inc. All rights reserved.

could be so difficult? How do Mom and Dad do it? How do they make it look so easy? I wouldn't have a chance to give my parents credit for all their hard work because in an instant, I was asleep.

© 2009 K12 Inc. All rights reserved.

© 2009 K12 Inc. All rights reserved.

so I offered to babysit for my sister. I've helped my parents take care of my sister since she was born four years ago, so I was sure that watching her alone would be a breeze. My parents agreed to my plan, but they warned me that it would be harder than I thought. I had no idea at the time how right they were.

When she finally did, I had to read it to her three times before she was satisfied. When I tried to turn off the lights, she started crying. How could I forget that she needed her nightlight? I had to sit with her for a few minutes to calm her down. Then I made sure to turn on her nightlight before turning off her room light. I closed her door behind me and let out a huge sigh.

My relief didn't last long. As soon as I stepped into the living room, I saw the mess. Toys were everywhere. My sister's movie was still playing. Then I realized I was still in wet clothes. I changed my clothes, turned off the movie, and cleaned up the mess. I sat on the couch and closed my eyes. Who knew taking care of a four-year-old

© 2009 K12 Inc. All rights reserved.

First, there was the running around the house. It didn't matter how many times I told my sister to stop running, she would not slow down. Each time I told her to stop, she stuck her tongue out at me and ran away. Before I knew it, I found myself running after her to try to make her listen to me. Some example I was setting! How can I ask my sister to stop running around the house if I'm running around after her?

Once my sister finally got tired, she decided she wanted to watch a movie. I thought that was a great idea because it meant she would sit still for a while. I turned on her favorite movie and sank into a chair as she watched the movie silently. I was barely able to catch my breath before she was up and moving

© 2009 K12 Inc. All rights reserved.

water. She splashed around for a while, and then she was ready to get out. It wasn't until after I dried her off that I realized I was soaking wet. My clothes were drenched from the water my sister splashed around while she was playing.

Changing into dry clothes would have to wait. We were already in the bathroom, so I figured now was the time to get her to brush her teeth. That was no easy task. My sister hates brushing her teeth. After a struggle that felt like it lasted forever, her teeth were finally brushed. A bedtime story and lights out were the only things left before I could finally relax!

Of course, my sister didn't make the end of the night easy for me. She couldn't decide on a bedtime story.

© 2009 K12 Inc. All rights reserved.

again. At least this time she was walking. I watched to see what she was going to do.

I wasn't surprised when she reached into her toy chest and pulled out her favorite dolls. She wanted me to play with her, so I sat down next to her on the floor. We played with her dolls for a few minutes before she headed back to the toy chest. This time, she pulled out her bucket of wooden blocks. She wanted me to build towers for her so she could knock them down. We spent a few minutes building and destroying block towers. Then she walked over to the toy chest again and dug out several puzzles. She wanted my help putting them together. When we finished the last puzzle, she walked back over to the toy chest. She came back with more

© 2009 K12 Inc. All rights reserved.

toys that we played with for only a few minutes. Back and forth my sister went to her toy chest. Before I knew it, all her toys were in a huge mess on the floor. I looked around the room in disbelief. How could one four-year-old make such a mess?

Just as I was going to ask her to start cleaning up, my sister told me she was ready for dinner. I didn't want my sister to get cranky because she was hungry, so I decided the mess could wait. I heated up dinner and listened to my sister chatter as we ate.

By the end of dinner, my sister was also a mess, so it was off to give her a bath. She wasn't happy until the bathtub was full of bubbles and all her bath toys were hidden under the

© 2009 K12 Inc. All rights reserved.

Unit 8 Assessment

Part 1.

On the lines provided, write the contractions formed by each set of two words that you are given.

1. they + will = _____

2. what + is = _____

3. you + would = _____

4. should + not = _____

5. let + us = _____

6. will + not = _____

7. she + will = _____

8. has + not = _____

Part 2.

On the lines provided, write the two words that make up each contraction given.

9. haven't = _____ + _____

10. he'll = _____ + _____

11. they'd = _____ + _____

12. they're = _____ + _____

13. it's = _____ + _____

14. they've = _____ + _____

15. we're = _____ + _____

16. could've = _____ + _____

© 2009 K12 Inc. All rights reserved.

Part 3.

On the lines provided, write each sentence that is read to you. Underline the contraction in each sentence.

17. _____

18. _____

19. _____

20. _____

21. _____

22. _____

23. _____

Part 4.

Underline the word or words that make the following sentences true.

24. A root word is a word part used to form a family of words with related meanings. A root word is different from a base word because a root word (is, is not) a word by itself.

25. A root word (can, cannot) stand alone.

© 2009 K12 Inc. All rights reserved.

Part 5.

Choose the root from the box that matches each clue. Write that root on the line provided.

cap	cred	sens

26. Which root given above means "to feel, perceive, or think"? _____

27. Which root given above means "to take"? _____

28. Which root given above means "to believe"? _____

Part 6.

Underline the word that best completes each sentence.

29. Carmine is very _____. He always makes good decisions.
    (sensible, creditor, captivating)

30. What a _____ song. I love the beat and the lyrics.
    (credence, sensational, captors)

31. Unable to go out because of the snow, I felt like a _____ in my own home.
    (captive, sensor, credential)

32. I always watch this new station because I feel the reporters are very _____.
    (sensed, capturing, credible)

© 2009 K12 Inc. All rights reserved.

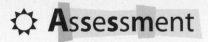
Part 7.

Draw lines from the words on the right to their definitions on the left.

33. belief, trust, praise, or approval   nonsense

to catch and hold by force or skill   captivate

words or actions that have no   incredible
meaning; foolishness

quick to feel or notice   credit

very great, unusual, or special   capture
in a way that makes it hard or
impossible to believe

to take someone's interest   sensitive

© 2009 K12 Inc. All rights reserved.

Get Ready

- Conjunctions connect words or groups of words. The three most common conjunctions are *and*, *but*, and *or*.

- A compound subject is two or more subjects, connected by a conjunction.

    Jeb *and* **Stan** are running in the race.

- Conjunctions also join verbs to form compound predicates. A compound predicate is two or more verbs joined by a conjunction.

    Jeb **ran** *and* **biked** in the race last year.

- In the sentence above, the compound predicate (two or more verbs connected by a conjunction) is "**ran** *and* **biked**." The two verbs (**ran**, **biked**) are joined by a conjunction (*and*).

© 2009 K12 Inc. All rights reserved.

Contractions and Root Word *sens*

Try It

Read each sentence. If the sentence contains a compound subject, write "CS" on the line provided. If the sentence contains a compound predicate, write "CP" on the line provided. In each sentence, circle the conjunction and underline the compound subject or compound predicate.

1. The babysitter is feeding Nicholas and dressing Nathan. _____

2. Sun but not heat is what I like. _____

3. She complained a lot but helped clean the barn. _____

4. The old car rattled and sputtered. _____

5. Spicy mustard or ketchup goes on my hamburger, not both. _____

6. I waved and yelled to get my friend's attention across the park.

   _____

7. Fresh goat's milk or juice tastes best with breakfast. _____

8. That sweetener but not sugar goes in my iced tea. _____

© 2009 K12 Inc. All rights reserved.

Sentence Completion

Choose the word from the box that best completes each sentence. Write each word on the line provided. Then read each sentence aloud.

masterpiece	supermarket	anywhere	campground
handshake	overlook	windshield	

1. A _____ is used as a greeting or a farewell.

2. We can go _____ you would like to go on Saturday.

3. If you build something without first reading the directions, you might _____ an important step.

4. When we drove in the mud, it splashed up and covered the _____ .

5. Nora studied the _____ carefully to try to learn how to improve her own paintings.

6. The _____ was full of shoppers buying food for their families.

7. My favorite _____ is in the mountains, about an hour from my house.

© 2009 K12 Inc. All rights reserved.

Using the Root *aud*

The root *aud* means "to hear." Choose a word from the box to match each phrase below. Write each word on the line provided.

| audio | audible | audience | audition | inaudible |

1. a group of people gathered to hear and see a performance _____

2. able to be heard _____

3. an opportunity for an actor, singer, or musician to test his or her talents by giving a short performance to be judged _____

4. having to do with what is heard on radio or television _____

5. unable to be heard _____

On the lines provided, write sentences using three of the words from the box above.

6. _____

_____

7. _____

_____

8. _____

_____

© 2009 K12 Inc. All rights reserved.

Hatching a Mystery

Paul was walking home from the animal hospital. It was summer, and he volunteered there three days a week. Paul liked working with all of the animals. He also liked learning from the veterinarians. As he walked the familiar path, Paul noticed something up ahead on the sidewalk. From a distance, it looked like a wadded-up brown bag. As Paul got closer, he realized that it wasn't

© 2009 K12 Inc. All rights reserved.

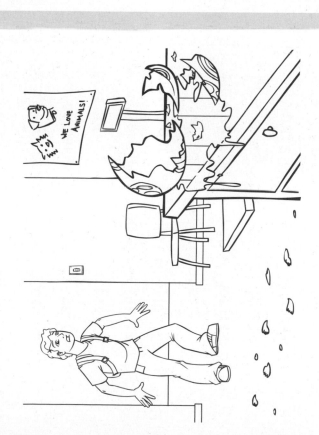

animal prints surrounded the eggshell. Paul followed the six-toed prints to a broken window. He peeked outside but found nothing. *Is this really happening?* Paul wondered. *Am I dreaming?* Just then, Paul got his answer.

© 2009 K12 Inc. All rights reserved.

a bag. *It must be a rock*, he thought. A few seconds later, Paul was looking down at the brown object. *That is*

definitely not a rock...

...mysterious item was about the size of a football. It was somewhat oval in shape and light brown with darker brown spots. Tiny blue dots were in the center of some of the dark brown spots. Paul had never seen anything like it, not even at the animal hospital. *It kind of looks like an egg*, Paul thought, *but what kind of an animal lays an egg like this?* Paul looked around for any clues. He was hoping to spot some strange animal lurking in the background. His search was unsuccessful. He didn't find a trace of any kind of animal, strange

knew more about the egg, or more specifically, about the animal inside the egg...

When he arrived at the hospital, he noticed it was eerily silent. He didn't hear any dogs barking or cats meowing. He didn't hear anyone talking on the phone. He didn't see any doctors walking around. "Hello?" Paul's voice echoed in the empty waiting room. He poked his head into several of the exam rooms and found them empty, too. His heart began to race as he got closer to the room with the egg. Paul pushed the door opened and looked inside the room. The egg was broken into three large pieces on the table. The box was on the floor. A trail of yellow, slimy

© 2009 K12 Inc. All rights reserved.

© 2009 K12 Inc. All rights reserved.

or normal. After looking around a little more, Paul decided he would put the egg in his backpack and take it to the animal hospital tomorrow. He pulled out an extra pair of hospital gloves and carefully picked up the egg. It was heavier than Paul expected. He put the egg to his ear and listened, but he didn't hear anything. Paul slid the egg carefully into his bag. His mind raced as he walked home. *What kind of egg is this? Where is the animal it came from? Is it even an egg?* he thought.

That night, Paul kept the egg in his bedroom. He carefully pulled it from his backpack and put it in a box on his desk. He studied the egg with a magnifying glass. He couldn't be sure, but he

© 2009 K12 Inc. All rights reserved.

longer than it had yesterday. Paul was not sure he wanted to meet the animal that hatched from that strange egg.

Before heading home for the day, Paul checked on the egg one last time. It had grown large enough to fill the entire box. The dark brown spots had spread so much that the entire egg was now dark brown. The tiny blue dots had also grown. Paul was glad to leave for the day. He left hoping the egg would be turned over to someone else by tomorrow.

That night, Paul couldn't sleep. His mind was going crazy with images of scary animals. When his alarm rang the next morning, Paul jumped out of bed. He wanted to get to the animal hospital early. He was hoping the doctors

© 2009 K12 Inc. All rights reserved.

thought the brown spots were a little bigger now. Paul covered the box before climbing into bed.

During the night, Paul was awakened by a scratching sound. He turned on his bedside light and looked toward his desk.

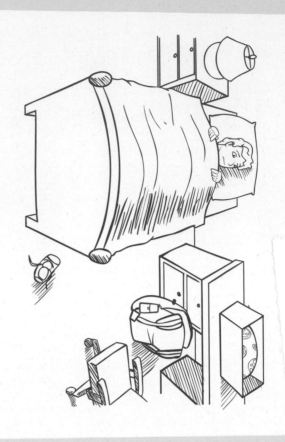

© 2009 K12 Inc. All rights reserved.

Was the scratching coming from the box? Did it just shake on his desk? Paul was definitely nervous now. He slept with the light on for the rest of the night.

The next day, Paul told the veterinarians about the egg. He pulled it from his backpack and watched their expressions change to shock. They touched the egg and listened to it. They looked through pictures in thick medical books. The doctors were just as confused as Paul. "We'll keep it here for now, but I think we need to report it to the city," the head doctor decided.

They left the egg in a box in one of the exam rooms. Paul checked on it throughout the day. He noticed the tiny blue dots were now on all of the dark brown spots. The egg also looked a little

© 2009 K12 Inc. All rights reserved.

Name:

Compound Words and Root Word *pend*

Match the Meaning

Choose the word from the box that matches each clue. Write each word on the line provided. Read aloud each word that you write.

countdown	driveway	checkbook
haircut	skyscraper	teammate

1. a book of checks _____

2. a very tall building _____

3. backwards counting that marks the _____
   time until the launch of a rocket or
   the start of an event

4. member of a team _____

Choose the word from the box above that best completes each sentence. Write each word on the line provided, then read each sentence aloud.

5. Each player on our team is assigned a _____ to work with during practice.

6. You can see the entire city from the deck on top of the

   _____ .

7. Many cars were parked in the _____ .

8. I went to the barber for a new _____ .

© 2009 K12 Inc. All rights reserved.

Using the Root Word *pend*

The root word *pend* means "to hang." Choose the word from the box that matches each phrase. Write each word on the line provided next to each phrase.

pendant   pendulum   suspend   pending

1. work that is hanging or unfinished

   1. _____

2. a locket or jewel that hangs from a necklace

   2. _____

3. a weight hung so that it swings back and forth

   3. _____

4. to hang something, usually from another object

   4. _____

Choose the word from the box above that best completes each sentence. Write each word on the lines provided. Then read each sentence aloud.

5. The necklace was gold, with a ruby _____ .

6. A decision about building a new playground at the local park is _____ .

7. The _____ on the clock has stopped swinging back and forth.

8. Ropes were used to _____ the worker while he repaired the power lines.

© 2009 K12 Inc. All rights reserved.

Not So Special Power

Paige dragged herself out of bed. It was Saturday morning, and she liked to sleep in as long as possible. This morning, however, her little brother had interrupted her plans. He decided to watch cartoons with the volume loud enough for the entire neighborhood to hear. The only thing louder than the television was the sound of his laughter. Paige had rolled over and covered her ears with her pillow to muffle the noise.

© 2009 K12 Inc. All rights reserved.

© 2009 K12 Inc. All rights reserved.

the next time she was ready to write. She looked over her last few entries and noticed some colored powder on the pages. Suddenly, it all made sense. "I knew that ring wasn't magic!" Paige shouted as she jumped out of bed. "Troy!"

Without even seeing his sister's face, Troy knew he'd been caught. His ring didn't have the power to get him out of this mess. "At least it was fun while it lasted!" he said, as he braced himself for his sister's tirade.

© 2009 K12 Inc. All rights reserved.

She had just drifted back into a deep sleep when she heard a crash from the kitchen. That's when she decided her sleep was officially over. She walked into the kitchen, barely picking her feet up with each step.

"What's going on in here, Troy?" she asked, scowling at her little brother. Her head was still groggy from sleep, but she wanted answers. "For a little kid, you sure make a lot of noise."

"I just made myself a bowl of cereal. I made a little mess when I dropped the milk, but I cleaned up everything," he said with a look of pride. He didn't seem at all concerned with his sister's angry tone.

© 2009 K12 Inc. All rights reserved.

journal was on top of her magazines. Paige always put her journal under her magazines. When she opened it to her last entry, she noticed her pencil was missing. Paige always left her pencil in her journal, so that it was there for

Paige rolled her eyes. She should have known. Her brother loved his cereal. He always ate the same kind, day after day. She was certain he would have eaten it for breakfast, lunch, and dinner, if their parents allowed it.

© 2009 K12 Inc. All rights reserved.

© 2009 K12 Inc. All rights reserved.

gave a sly smile, waved his ring at her, and ran off after his ball.

That night, Paige was practicing her piano music. "You better make sure you practice extra hard," Troy suggested. "You don't want to mess up on your piano test tomorrow."

Paige was confused. She was certain she had never told Troy about her headache, or losing her earring, or her piano test. She knew there was no such thing as magic, but she was starting to wonder. Did Troy's ring really have special powers?

After brushing her teeth, Paige climbed into bed. She opened the drawer of her bedside table to pull out her journal. She noticed that her

"Cool! A magic ring!" Troy exclaimed. As usual, his face and hands were covered with powder from the marshmallows in his cereal. He waved the trinket around like a prize. "I just found it in my cereal. The box says this ring will give me special powers."

"Troy, you don't honestly believe a ring from your cereal box is magic, do you? There's no such thing as magic," Paige said. She frowned at the thought of her brother believing such a silly thing.

"You'll see," Troy responded, as he waved his hand and walked out of the kitchen.

Later that evening, Paige was sitting on her bed reading a book. Troy poked

his head into her room. "How's your head?" he asked. "Does it still hurt?"

Paige gave him a strange look. "Um, it's fine," she replied. "I don't remember telling you I had a headache." Troy just shrugged his shoulders, waved his ring at her, and continued walking.

The next day, Paige was helping her mother in the garden when Troy ran by, chasing his ball. He stopped for a minute to talk with his mother and Paige. Before walking away, he looked at Paige and asked her if she found her favorite earring that she had lost. "Troy, I know I never told you about losing my earring. Have you been eavesdropping when I'm talking on the phone?" she accused. Troy

© 2009 K12 Inc. All rights reserved.

© 2009 K12 Inc. All rights reserved.

Find the Compound Words

Read each sentence. Find and underline each compound word.
Then read each sentence aloud.

1. I have an art book with pictures of famous masterpieces.

2. The supermarket advertised special prices in the newspaper.

3. We used firewood to build a campfire each night of our camping trip.

4. My brother and I have a secret handshake that no one else knows.

5. I was careful not to overlook my bookshelf when I dusted my room.

6. Elena gave her father a new billfold for his birthday.

7. My grandparents are coming to visit for three weeks this summer.

8. Raymond was outstanding in the lead role of the play.

9. We always buy peppermint flavored candy during winter.

10. Studying for the history test was worthwhile because I earned a perfect score!

Write four more compound words on the lines provided below.

11. _____

12. _____

13. _____

14. _____

© 2009 K12 Inc. All rights reserved.

Using the Root Word *ten*

The root word *ten* means "to stretch." Choose a word from the box to match each phrase below. Write each word on the line provided.
Hint: One word will be used twice.

antenna	extend	tension	tent

1. to stretch out or make longer _____

2. one of the pair of sense organs found on the _____
    head of insects, crabs, or lobsters

3. a shelter of fabric stretched over poles and _____
    attached to stakes

4. the condition of stretching or being stretched, _____
    or an anxious feeling

5. a wire or set of wires that extends or stretches _____
    out to send and receive radio waves

Choose the word from the box above that best completes each sentence below. Write each word on the line provided. Then read each sentence aloud.

6. When we go camping, we will sleep in a _____ .

7. The long _____ on the radio will help pick up the signal.

8. You could feel the _____ in the crowd as they waited for
    the player to take the free throw.

9. You will need to _____ the ladder all the way to reach
    the second floor.

© 2009 K12 Inc. All rights reserved.

Get Ready

- Conjunctions connect words or groups of words. The three most common conjunctions are *and*, *but*, and *or*.

- A compound direct object is two or more direct objects, connected by a conjunction. The direct object answers the questions *whom* or *what* after the action verb.

I will call **Jen** *or* **Beth** and ask directions.

Whom did I call? Jen, Beth. The conjunction *or* lets us connect the two direct objects.

I bought **shirts** *and* **shoes** at the mall.

What did I buy? Shirts, shoes. The conjunction *and* lets us connect the two direct objects.

© 2009 K12 Inc. All rights reserved.

Try It

Complete the sentences by writing appropriate words on the lines provided.

1. The role of a conjunction is to _____ words or groups of words.

2. Conjunctions can form _____ subjects, predicates, or direct objects.

3. The three most common conjunctions are _____ .

Circle the conjunction in each sentence below. Underline the direct objects that each conjunction connects.

4. Tonight, Dad is cooking macaroni and cheese for dinner.

5. Would you like to drink milk or water with dinner?

6. We bought not cake but ice cream for dessert.

7. Please clear the dishes and cups from the table.

8. Please help Jack and Shawn with the dishes.

© 2009 K12 Inc. All rights reserved.

Words Within Words and Root Word *lect*

Match the Meaning

Choose a word from the box to match each clue. Write each word in the second column. Write the shorter form of the word in the third column. Read aloud each word that you write.

necktie	dormitory	gymnasium	fanatic	examination

1. test _____ _____

2. building or room used for exercises or games _____ _____

3. person who takes a great interest in something _____ _____

4. cloth band worn around the neck and tied in front _____ _____

5. building at college or boarding school with rooms for people to live and sleep in _____ _____

© 2009 K12 Inc. All rights reserved.

Word **W**ork

Name:

Words Within Words and Root Word *lect*

Using the Root Word *lect*

The root word *lect* means "to choose." Choose a word from the box to match each phrase below. Write that word on the line provided.

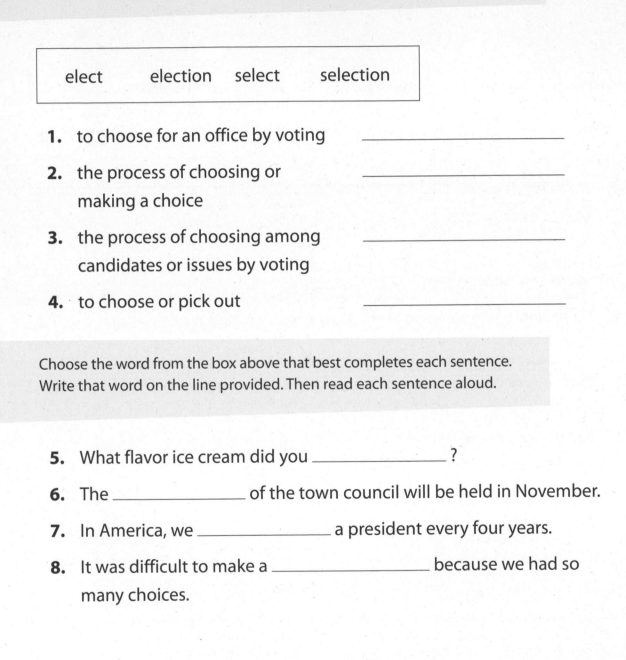

| elect | election | select | selection |

1. to choose for an office by voting _____

2. the process of choosing or making a choice _____

3. the process of choosing among candidates or issues by voting _____

4. to choose or pick out _____

Choose the word from the box above that best completes each sentence. Write that word on the line provided. Then read each sentence aloud.

5. What flavor ice cream did you _____ ?

6. The _____ of the town council will be held in November.

7. In America, we _____ a president every four years.

8. It was difficult to make a _____ because we had so many choices.

© 2009 K12 Inc. All rights reserved.

From Fan to Friend

"It looks like someone is finally moving in next door," Nick's mom said. "It's been empty for so long. It'll be nice to have neighbors again." The house next door had been empty for almost a year. It used to belong to the Drake family, until they moved away for Mrs. Drake's new job. Nick grew up playing with Gabe. They played ball in their backyards. They rode their bikes around the neighborhood. They played

© 2009 K12 Inc. All rights reserved.

As Blake's father was explaining their decision, Blake noticed Nick's baseball bat and glove by the door. "Hey, Nick, what do you say we leave the adults to talk about the boring stuff, and we head to your backyard to play some baseball?" Blake suggested.

Nick agreed immediately. He couldn't believe he was about to play baseball with Blake Alba! As they walked to the backyard, they talked about their favorite baseball teams. While they played, they talked about their favorite players. The more Nick got to know Blake, the more he realized he really was just a normal kid. Nick was excited to learn they had many things in common, except the movie star thing!

© 2009 K12 Inc. All rights reserved.

video games on rainy days. Nick never considered how life would be without his friend next door. He was sad to find out that they were moving, and even sadder living next door to an empty house for the past months. Still, he wasn't sure he was looking forward to someone else moving in next door.

"I guess it'll be nice to have neighbors again," he replied. "I just wish those neighbors were the Drakes." He walked over to the window to see if he could catch a glimpse of the new family. He saw a moving van and a woman and man unloading it. They made several trips in and out of the house before they noticed Nick watching them. They turned to face the window and gave a

© 2009 K12 Inc. All rights reserved.

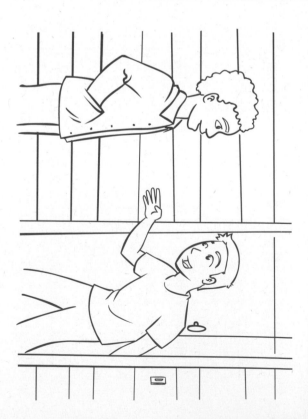

looking for," Vince said. "We wanted to live someplace quiet. As you can see, we have someone in the family that people are pretty excited to meet. Besides the fact that Blake acts in movies, we really are a normal family. This neighborhood seems like a place where we can relax and live a normal life."

© 2009 K12 Inc. All rights reserved.

friendly wave. Nick waved back. "They seem nice enough," he said. "I haven't seen any kids, though."

"Nick, get away from the window. We don't want the new neighbors to think we're sn... " his mom scolded. "I guess since they've already seen you,

© 2009 K12 Inc. All rights reserved.

Nick's face. "Hi, Nick. I'm Blake," he said, introducing himself casually.

"I know who you are!" Blake shouted excitedly. "You're my favorite actor. I can't believe you're standing on my porch!"

Nick's mother joined the group at the front door. She took one look at Blake and knew Nick must have been in complete shock. "So this is Blake," she said, extending her hand for a shake. "You've already met your biggest fan. I'm his mother, Kim."

After a few speechless minutes, Nick was finally back to himself. He told his new neighbors that he was surprised they would choose to move into the house next door, instead of a fancy house in a big city. "Actually, this neighborhood is exactly what we were

© 2009 K12 Inc. All rights reserved.

we should go introduce ourselves." Nick and his mother walked next door. As they were approaching the open front door, the man and woman moving in saw them, smiled, and started walking toward them. Nick thought he saw someone else slip into the next room. "Hi, we're your neighbors," Nick's mom said, extending her hand for a handshake. "I'm Kim, and this is my son Nick."

"It's nice to meet you. I'm Vince, and this is my wife Sue," the man responded. "Our son Blake is around here somewhere. He's about your age, Nick. It's moving day and he's trying to do as little work as possible!" Everyone laughed at the comment. They all talked for a few minutes. Kim offered help if

they needed it, and then she and Nick returned to their house.

"Looks like you might have a new friend after all," Nick's mom said. "Let's hope you'll meet him soon."

"I thought I saw him slip into the next room when we walked up to the door. I don't know why, but he looked a little familiar," Nick replied.

The next day, Nick and his mother were in the kitchen when they heard a knock on their front door. Nick opened the door and was immediately face to face with his favorite actor, Blake Alba! Vince and Sue were standing behind Blake. They gave a knowing smile when they saw the look of shock on

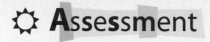

Assessment

Name:

Unit 9 Assessment

Part 1.

Listen to each word that is read to you. Write that word on the line provided.

1. _____

2. _____

3. _____

4. _____

5. _____

6. _____

7. _____

8. _____

9. _____

10. _____

Part 2.

Underline the compound word in each group.

11.	absent	accident	anteater
12.	weekly	winter	without
13.	backpack	battery	beginner
14.	talented	toothbrush	tractor
15.	cabinet	cookbook	costume

© 2009 K12 Inc. All rights reserved.

Part 3.

Read each definition below. Underline the root word that matches each definition.

16. Definition: to hear

Root Words: aud, form, lect, pend, ten, vita

17. Definition: to shape or outline

Root Words: aud, form, lect, pend, ten, vita

18. Definition: to hang

Root Words: aud, form, lect, pend, ten, vita

19. Definition: to stretch

Root Words: aud, form, lect, pend, ten, vita

20. Definition: to choose

Root Words: aud, form, lect, pend, ten, vita

21. Definition: life

Root Words: aud, form, lect, pend, ten, vita

Part 4.

Listen to each word that is read to you. Write each word on the lines provided in the first column. Then write the shorter form of the word in the second column.

22. _____   _____

23. _____   _____

24. _____   _____

25. _____   _____

26. _____   _____

27. _____   _____

© 2009 K12 Inc. All rights reserved.

Part 5.

Underline the compound word or compound words in each sentence.

28. My father greets everyone with a handshake.

29. We drove up to the overlook to take pictures of the city below.

30. The motorcycle driver wore a helmet for safety.

31. We watched the newscast to learn more about the water shortage in our town.

32. The singer gave an outstanding performance, so the audience gave him a standing ovation.

33. My grandfather served us peppermint flavored ice cream for dessert.

34. I cheered wildly when my teammate hit a home run!

35. I waited all afternoon for the mail to arrive.

36. The dog scratched on the backdoor because she wanted to come inside.

37. We told ghost stories around the campfire before we went to sleep.

© 2009 K12 Inc. All rights reserved.

Part 6.

Choose the word from the box that best completes each sentence below. Write that word on the line provided.

| audition election formula pendant tent revitalize |

38. The _____ was large enough to fit five sleeping bags.

39. The city is working to _____ local parks and playgrounds.

40. Calvin talked to his parents about who they voted for in the

_____ .

41. Jenny's favorite _____ was once part of her grandmother's necklace.

42. I used the _____ to determine the correct answer to the math problem.

43. The actress introduced herself to the judges before she began her

_____ .

© 2009 K12 Inc. All rights reserved.

Homophones

Choose a word from the box to match each clue. Write each word in the second column. Read aloud each word that you write.

berry	groan	mail	tail	waist
bury	grown	male	tale	waste

1. to place in the ground and cover   _____

2. material that is thrown away   _____

3. to have become larger or increased   _____

4. a story   _____

5. a man or a boy   _____

6. a deep sound that shows sorrow, pain, annoyance, or disapproval   _____

7. small fruit   _____

8. the rear part of an animal   _____

9. something carried in the postal system   _____

10. the part of the body between the ribs and hips   _____

© 2009 K12 Inc. All rights reserved.

Using the Root Word *divi*

The root word *divi* means "to divide." Choose a word from the box that means the same or almost the same as the underlined word or words in each sentence. Write each word on the line provided below.

| divide   division   individual   indivisible |

1. The "Pledge of Allegiance" describes America as a nation that is <u>not able to be separated</u>.

    _____

2. <u>Separate</u> the cupcakes among the guests.

    _____

3. The <u>person</u> was wearing a white shirt and black pants.

    _____

4. He made an equal <u>separation</u> of blocks among the four children.

    _____

On the lines provided below, write sentences using two words from the box above. Then read each sentence aloud.

5. _____

    _____

6. _____

    _____

© 2009 K12 Inc. All rights reserved.

Wish You
Were Here

"It's really bittersweet, Grandpa. I always go to visit you on your birthday, but this year my art club is taking a trip. The trip is the same weekend as your birthday, so I won't be able to celebrate with you," Cora explained. "I'm really excited about the art club trip, but I'm really sad about your birthday."

© 2009 K12 Inc. All rights reserved.

her grandfather. She gave it to Cora and watched as Cora's eyes filled with tears of happiness. Looking back at her was the picture of her parents and her grandfather holding the sign he had made. The sign read, "Thank you, Cora! Wish you were here!"

© 2009 K12 Inc. All rights reserved.

"Don't be sad," Grandpa replied. "Your art trip is important. You've been a member of the club for years. You're very interested in art. This is a great way for you to learn more about it. Enjoy yourself!"

Cora talked with her grandfather for a few more minutes. When they hung up, she still felt sad. Her grandfather lived in another state, so she didn't get to see him very often. She always liked visiting for his birthday because she got to make up for lost time. He would ask her about everything in her life, and she would ask him about everything in his. They would spend hours telling each other stories

© 2009 K12 Inc. All rights reserved.

of Cora with her art club in front of an art museum. Cora held a sign that read, "Happy birthday, Grandpa! Wish you were here!"

"This is the best gift I've ever received," Grandpa said, wiping away his tears. "I know just how to thank her." He found a pen and a piece of paper and made a sign. Then he grabbed his camera and set it on a tripod. He set the timer on his camera. Then he and Cora's parents sat on the couch. Grandpa held up his sign just in time for the photograph.

When Cora returned home, she told her parents all about her trip and they told her about theirs. Then Cora's mother pulled out a card from

© 2009 K12 Inc. All rights reserved.

and working in Grandpa's woodshop. The days always flew by when Cora visited her grandfather.

Cora's mother could see the disappointment in Cora's face. "Cora, I know you're sad about missing your grandfather's birthday, but try to stay positive. You're going to have a great time exploring a new city!" she said encouragingly. "You'll get to visit different art museums. You'll also get to paint different landscapes and scenery that you don't have here. Make sure you take plenty of pictures of your trip, and we'll do the same."

"That's it!" Cora exclaimed. "You just gave me the perfect idea for

© 2009 K12 Inc. All rights reserved.

HAPPY BIRTHDAY GRANDPA!
WISH YOU WERE HERE!

he found the album Cora had made for him. He looked through all the pictures. He laughed at the silly ones, just as Cora knew he would. When he got to the last page, Grandpa's eyes began to water. There, on the last page, was a picture

© 2009 K12 Inc. All rights reserved.

Grandpa's birthday gift. He's not here to see everything that goes on around here, since he lives so far away. I'll look through the pictures I've taken this year and make a photo album for him. He's going to love it!"

Cora spent the next two weeks making her grandfather's photo album. She loved looking through all of the photographs she'd taken during the last year. She chose silly pictures and serious pictures. She included pictures from family trips and photos taken around their house. She knew her grandfather would love looking at everything she and her family did all year. When she finished the album, she packed it in her suitcase to take with her on the art trip.

© 2009 K12 Inc. All rights reserved.

"Cora, would you like us to give Grandpa his photo album when we see him?" her father asked.

"No, thanks. I'm going to mail it while I'm on my trip," Cora answered.

Several days later, Cora's parents were sitting with her grandfather at his house. They were talking about how much they missed Cora and wished she had been able to visit with them. Just then, the doorbell rang. It was the postal worker delivering the mail. She was holding a package too large to fit inside Grandpa's mailbox. Grandpa smiled and thanked her for the delivery.

"This looks like Cora's handwriting," he said as he opened the package. Inside

© 2009 K12 Inc. All rights reserved.

Name: _____

Homophones and Base Word *grace*

Practice with Homophones

Choose a word from the box that means the same or almost the same as the word or words below. Write each word in the second column. Read aloud each word that you write

close	dear	hear	heard	our
clothes	deer	here	herd	hour

1. listen _____

2. shut _____

3. precious _____

4. garment or apparel _____

5. some groups of animals _____

6. sensed by the ears _____

Choose a word from the box above to match each clue below. Write each word in the second column. Read aloud each word that you write.

7. You might find this animal in a meadow or forest. _____

8. This means something that belongs to us. _____

9. This is made up of sixty minutes. _____

10. Come to this place instead of going there. _____

© 2009 K12 Inc. All rights reserved.

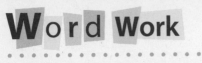

Name:

Using the Base Word *grace*

Choose a word from the box to match each phrase below. Write each word in the second column.

grace	graceful	gracious	disgrace

1. having or behaving in a kind and pleasant manner _____

2. a charming or pleasant manner _____

3. someone or something that causes shame or the loss of pleasing qualities _____

4. full of or having a charming or pleasant manner _____

Choose the word from the box above that best completes each sentence. Write each word on the line provided. Then read each sentence aloud.

5. She acted with _____ when she lost the spelling bee to her best friend.

6. The house with the overgrown yard was a _____ to the neighborhood.

7. He was a very _____ party host who always made sure we were enjoying ourselves.

8. The _____ figure skater glided across the ice.

© 2009 K12 Inc. All rights reserved.

312

Get Ready

- Conjunctions connect words or groups of words. The three most common conjunctions are *and*, *but*, and *or*.

- A compound sentence is two or more sentences connected by a conjunction. When you combine two sentences, you must replace the end punctuation of the first sentence with a comma.

- Look at these sentences. Each sentence in part B is a compound sentence created by combining the two separate sentences in part A.

> **A.** Luke has a python. He keeps it in a cage.
>
> **B.** Luke has a python, **and** he keeps it in a cage.
>
> **A.** I don't know if I'd like a snake as a pet. It's easy to take care of.
>
> **B.** I don't know if I'd like a snake as a pet, **but** it's easy to take care of.
>
> **A.** Luke might take his snake with him. Joe might take care of the snake for Luke while he's away.
>
> **B.** Luke might take his snake with him, **or** Joe might take care of the snake for Luke while he's away.

Notice that in each part B, the two sentences are joined first by a comma and then by a conjunction.

- The conjunction *and* joins ideas that are alike or similar; the conjunction *but* joins ideas that are different or contrasting; and the conjunction *or* joins ideas that are choices or alternatives.

© 2009 K12 Inc. All rights reserved.

Try It

Write the word or words that complete each sentence on the lines provided.

1. The role of a conjunction is to _____ words or groups of words.

2. Conjunctions can make _____ subjects, predicates, direct objects, or sentences.

3. The three most common conjunctions are _____ , _____ , and _____ .

On the lines provided, rewrite the following pairs of sentences as compound sentences.

I have piano lessons at 4 p.m. today. I didn't practice.

_____

_____

5. I have played the piano since I was 5. I have played the flute since I was 10.

_____

_____

6. When she's older, my little sister would like to play the piano. She might play the drums.

_____

_____

© 2009 K12 Inc. All rights reserved.

Code **W**ork

Name: ....

Homophones and Base Word *deficit*

Homophones

Choose a word from the box to match each clue below. Write that word on the line provided. Read aloud each word that you write.

chews	days	pause	presence	rose
choose	daze	paws	presents	rows

1. to select _____

2. gifts _____

3. the feet of a four-footed animal _____

4. horizontal lines of objects _____

5. 24-hour periods that begin at midnight _____

6. fact or condition of being here or at a certain place _____

7. a state of being stunned or dizzy _____

8. a brief stop _____

9. a flower or the past tense of rise _____

10. grinds with the teeth _____

© 2009 K12 Inc. All rights reserved.

Using the Base Word *deficit*

Choose a word from the box to match each phrase below. Write that word on the line provided.

| deficit   deficient   deficiency |

1. an adjective meaning "not having enough" _____

2. a shortage, especially when referring to money _____

3. a noun meaning "a lack or shortage of something" _____

Choose a word from the box above to complete each sentence below. Write that word on the line provided. Then read each sentence aloud.

4. Taxes had to be raised to make up for the large _____ in the state budget.

5. If your diet is _____ in calcium, you have a risk of developing weak bones as you age.

6. Someone suffering from iron _____ may feel weak and tired.

© 2009 K12 Inc. All rights reserved.

The Crocodile and the Beavers

There once was a crocodile that lived in a swamp. His skin was green and bumpy. His teeth were long and sharp. None of the other animals wanted to be his friend. They were afraid of the crocodile. They thought he would try to eat them. They didn't know he was nice and friendly, and tired of being lonely. He wanted nothing more than to meet them and spend his days at the swamp with friends.

© 2009 K12 Inc. All rights reserved.

---

did not want to hurt the beavers. He was trying to help them!

The crocodile delivered the beavers safely to the shore. All of the animals cheered. The baby beavers and their mother thanked the crocodile. All of the animals apologized to the crocodile for ignoring him in the past. They realized that they had let his large size and sharp teeth scare them. They hadn't taken the time to get to know the crocodile because of the way he looked. From that day on, the crocodile never spent a lonely day in the swamp again. He was always surrounded by friends who didn't let what he looked like on the outside, keep them from enjoying the wonderful crocodile on the inside.

© 2009 K12 Inc. All rights reserved.

One day, while the crocodile was swimming, he heard a strange sound. He looked around. Three baby beavers were wandering alone. They looked lost and scared. The crocodile could see the babies needed help. Without thinking twice, he took them to his house. When they arrived, the crocodile sat down to think. It was time for dinner, but he didn't know what to feed them. He asked the babies what they liked to eat, but they were no help. They were busy climbing up the crocodile's tail and onto his back. Their giggles filled his house. They liked playing with the big green crocodile, and he liked playing with them. It was nice to have animals around that weren't afraid of him. When

© 2009 K12 Inc. All rights reserved.

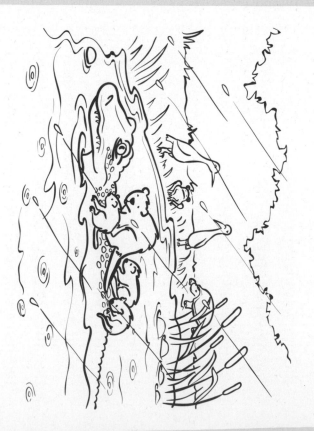

into the water. His big, heavy body was strong enough to fight the current. He quickly reached the frightened beavers. he crocodile waited calmly as the three babies led their mother onto his back. The other animals watched in surprise. They had misjudged the crocodile. He

© 2009 K12 Inc. All rights reserved.

the baby beavers grew hungry, they finally told the crocodile that they ate tree bark. The crocodile left to gather dinner for the babies. When he returned, his arms were full of bark. The babies ate it all. When they finished eating, everyone fell asleep.

© 2009 K12 Inc. All rights reserved.

---

them. He could help the babies find their mother after the storm. Just as he and the babies turned to go back to his house, the other animals trapped the crocodile with a net!

During all the fuss, no one noticed the baby beavers rush towards the water. The babies did not realize the storm had created a very strong current. When they jumped into the swamp, they were unable to swim in the rough waters. The babies started floating further and further away. At that moment, their mother appeared. She jumped into the water to save her babies, but the current was also too powerful for her. The crocodile knew exactly what he had to do. He used his sharp teeth to cut through the net. Then he hurried

© 2009 K12 Inc. All rights reserved.

The next day, the crocodile came up with a plan. He was going to help his new friends find their mother. He fed the baby beavers bark for breakfast. Then he and the babies left his house to begin their search. Many of the other animals were also awake and crowded around the swamp. When they saw the crocodile with the baby beavers, they immediately thought the worst. They were certain that the crocodile would hurt the babies. Something had to be done. They decided to rescue the babies and return them to their mother.

Perhaps if the animals had taken the time to watch the crocodile with the baby beavers, they would have realized there was no need to worry. They would have seen the babies

© 2009 K12 Inc. All rights reserved.

laughing and playing. Perhaps if the animals had asked the crocodile why the beavers were with him, then all the misunderstanding could have been avoided. The other animals, however, did not pay attention. They did not talk to the crocodile. Instead, they put their plan in motion.

While the animals prepared their rescue, no one noticed that the sky had turned gray. A storm was coming. Small raindrops began to fall. Soon hard rain pounded the swamp. The wind whipped through the trees. Lightning filled the sky. Thunder roared. The crocodile knew that thi was a dangerous situation. He d d to take the baby beavers to a place. He wanted to protect

© 2009 K12 Inc. All rights reserved.

Homophones

Choose a word from the box to match each clue below. Write that word on the line provided. Read aloud each word that you write.

allowed	fined	guessed	missed	towed
aloud	find	guest	mist	toad

1. visitor _____

2. pulled _____

3. discover _____

4. imagined _____

5. permitted _____

6. overlooked _____

7. haze of water _____

8. charged money _____

9. animal similar to a frog _____

10. spoken with a normal voice _____

© 2009 K12 Inc. All rights reserved.

Name:

Using the Root Word *grad*

The root word *grad* means "step, stage, degree, or rank." Choose a word from the box to match each clue below. Write that word on the line provided and read each word aloud.

Hint: Two of the words will be used more than once.

degrade	grade	gradual	graduate

1. degree of incline on a road or hill _____

2. changing by regular or continuous degrees _____

3. to remove or lower in quality, degree, or rank _____

4. to advance to a new level of skill, achievement, or activity _____

5. an indication of a person's rank in a subject studied at school or university _____

6. a person who has received a degree or diploma from a school or university _____

Choose a word from the box above that best completes each sentence. Write that word on the line provided. Then read each sentence aloud.

7. My brother will _____ from college in June.

8. Thanks to hours of studying, I received a high _____ on my exam.

© 2009 K12 Inc. All rights reserved.

Get Ready

- **Subjects:** The *subject* of a sentence is *who* or *what* the sentence is about. The *complete subject* is a noun or pronoun and all of its modifiers. The most important word in the subject is the noun or pronoun. This noun or pronoun is called the *simple subject*. Sometimes the subject and the simple subject are the same. To find a subject, ask "Who?" or "What?" about the verb.

Sentence	Ask	Simple Subject
Sally rode her bike.	Who or what rode?	Sally
She wore a helmet.	Who or what wore?	She

- **Predicates:** The *predicate* of a sentence tells more about what the subject is or does. The *complete predicate* contains the verb and all its modifiers, direct objects, or subject complements. The most important word in the predicate is the verb, which is also called the *simple predicate*. Sometimes the predicate and the simple predicate are the same. To find a predicate, ask, "What does the sentence tell about the subject?"

Sentence	Complete Predicate	Verb/Simple Predicate
Sally rode her bike.	…rode her bike	rode
She wore a helmet.	…wore a helmet	wore

- **Direct Objects:** The *direct object* of a sentence is a noun or pronoun that completes the action of the verb. To find the direct object of a sentence, ask "Whom?" or "What?" after the verb. The noun or pronoun that answers that question is the direct object. Remember, however, that only sentences with action verbs can have direct objects.

Sentence	Ask	Direct Object
Sally rode her bike.	Rode what?	her bike
She wore a helmet.	Wore what?	a helmet

© 2009 K12 Inc. All rights reserved.

Try It

Read each sentence. Identify the simple subject, simple predicate, and direct object, and write each on the lines provided.

1. Ethan, my friend, wrote a book.

Simple subject: _____

Simple predicate: _____

Direct object: _____

2. Jacob and Jessica play the piano.

Simple subject: _____

Simple predicate: _____

Direct object: _____

3. They won the game.

Simple subject: _____

Simple predicate: _____

Direct object: _____

4. Maya practices karate.

Simple subject: _____

Simple predicate: _____

Direct object: _____

5. She has a black belt.

Simple subject: _____

Simple predicate: _____

Direct object: _____

© 2009 K12 Inc. All rights reserved.

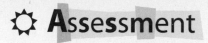
Unit 10 Assessment

Part 1.

Underline the homophone in parentheses that completes each sentence.

1. I was (find, fined) because the book was overdue.
2. The (toad, towed) has bumpy skin.
3. The rain fell as a fine (missed, mist).
4. I am bringing my cousin to the pool as my (guessed, guest).
5. My sister and I like to read (allowed, aloud) to each other.
6. We recycle (waist, waste) to save the environment.
7. The squirrel will (berry, bury) the nuts in the garden.

Part 2.

Underline the homophones in each group below.

8.	saw	say	sew	so
9.	road	rod	rode	rowed
10.	lessen	lesson	listen	loosen
11.	their	there	there's	they're
12.	weak	week	whack	wheat
13.	mail	male	mall	meal
14.	grain	green	groan	grown
15.	close	clot	cloth	clothes

© 2009 K12 Inc. All rights reserved.

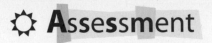
Part 3.

Listen to each sentence that is read to you. On the line provided, write the correct homophone in each sentence.

16. _____

17. _____

18. _____

19. _____

20. _____

21. _____

22. _____

Part 4.

Listen to each pair of homophones that is read to you. Write the homophones on the lines provided.

23. _____   _____

24. _____   _____

25. _____   _____

26. _____   _____

27. _____   _____

28. _____   _____

29. _____   _____

30. _____   _____

© 2009 K12 Inc. All rights reserved.

> ## Part 5.
>
> Read each definition below. Underline the correct base word or root word from the second line that matches each definition.

31. Definition: to divide

deficit, divi, grace, grad, prehend

32. Definition: a charming or pleasant manner

deficit, divi, grace, grad, prehend

33. Definition: a shortage

deficit, divi, grace, grad, prehend

34. Definition: step, stage, degree, or rank

deficit, divi, grace, grad, prehend

35. Definition: seize or grasp

deficit, divi, grace, grad, prehend

© 2009 K12 Inc. All rights reserved.

Part 6.

Choose a word from the box that best completes each sentence below.
Write that word on the line provided.

comprehend	deficient	divide	gracious	graduate

36. My sister is always _____ when she wins awards.

37. My cousin will _____ from college with a degree in biology.

38. I had to _____ the toys equally between my two little brothers.

39. The movie was in another language, so I could not _____ the story.

40. A person who eats plenty of fruits and vegetables will not be _____ in important vitamins.

© 2009 K12 Inc. All rights reserved.

The Schwa Sound

The schwa sound in six words in the box is spelled with the letter *a* and sounds like a short *u*. Underline the six words that contain the schwa sound spelled with letter *a*. Then use each of those words to complete one of the sentences below. Write each word on the line provided.

apple	alarm	asked	pasta	aroma
gray	cinema	pizza	drama	after

1. We bought some _____ noodles and vegetables to make for dinner.

2. There is a new movie playing at the _____ that I would really like to see.

3. I set the car _____ off by accident, and it made a loud, beeping noise.

4. My _____ club is getting ready for its new play to start next week.

5. I jumped up to open the door for the _____ delivery person.

6. The wonderful _____ coming from the kitchen made my mouth water.

© 2009 K12 Inc. All rights reserved.

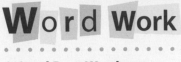

Name:

The Root Word *tox*

Each sentence below contains a word formed from the root word *tox*.
Circle the word with the root word *tox*. In each word, underline the root
word *tox*. Find and circle each of the four words in the word search.
Words may appear across, down, diagonally, or backward.

1. Most children's shampoos are nontoxic, and are not harmful
   if swallowed.

2. This plant contains a toxin that, if eaten by a cat, can make
   the animal very sick.

3. Dr. Evans reviewed the toxicology report to see what was
   making her patient ill.

4. The workers wore special masks to keep from inhaling the
   toxic fumes.

l	g	t	o	x	i	c	z	o	g	c
o	c	i	r	n	a	n	y	f	h	a
g	h	t	w	l	d	o	g	g	c	s
y	i	e	o	o	a	n	o	o	k	l
t	k	i	p	x	m	f	l	o	i	w
o	n	s	o	c	i	o	o	g	d	o
x	c	o	g	h	e	n	c	n	g	g
c	o	c	r	c	y	p	i	c	i	o
n	s	y	w	n	c	o	x	o	m	n
i	n	g	o	o	h	a	o	d	z	p
x	n	x	c	i	x	o	t	n	o	n

© 2009 K12 Inc. All rights reserved.

Crossword: The Schwa Sound /ə/

Read the clues to fill in the crossword.
Hint: Each correct answer will either begin or end with the schwa sound spelled with the letter *a*.

Across

3. spaghetti

5. fearful

6. underwater breathing equipment

8. the capacity, talent, or power to do something

10. the opposite of together

11. another name for mountain lion or panther

Down

1. a pleasant scent or sme[ll]

2. information

4. a type of mathematics where letters and other symbo[ls] represent quantities

7. to try

9. a play

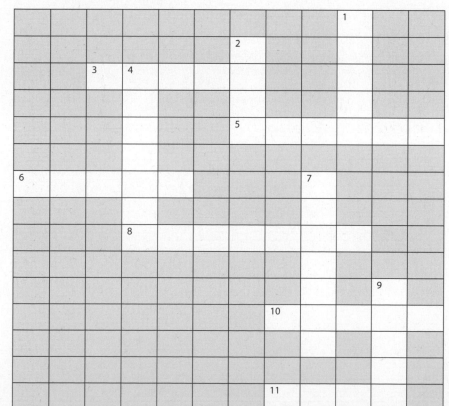

© 2009 K12 Inc. All rights reserved.

The Root Word *tech*

In each sentence, circle the word formed from the root word *tech*. Then underline the root word *tech* in each word.

1. The ice skater's technique was flawless, so no one was surprised when she won first place.

2. The technician came to investigate the problem with our Internet connection.

3. Computer technology has come a long way in a very short amount of time.

4. While I didn't understand all of the technical terms he used, I still understood the scientist's lecture.

Which Is Which?

Three of the words above that contain the root word *tech* are nouns and one word is an adjective. In the sentences below, write the correct words with the root word *tech* on the lines provided. Use these hints to complete the sentences below:

• A noun is a person, place, thing, or idea.
• An adjective is a word that describes a noun.

5. The three nouns are _____ ,
    _____ , and _____ .

6. The one adjective is _____ .

© 2009 K12 Inc. All rights reserved.

Memories, Old and New

Amber and Walt walked up to their front porch. Walt pulled out his key and unlocked the door to their house. They were a bit startled to find a stranger asleep on their father's recliner. They were whispering about what they should do when the man opened his eyes. "Oh, hello. You must be Amber and Walt," he said.

© 2009 K12 Inc. All rights reserved.

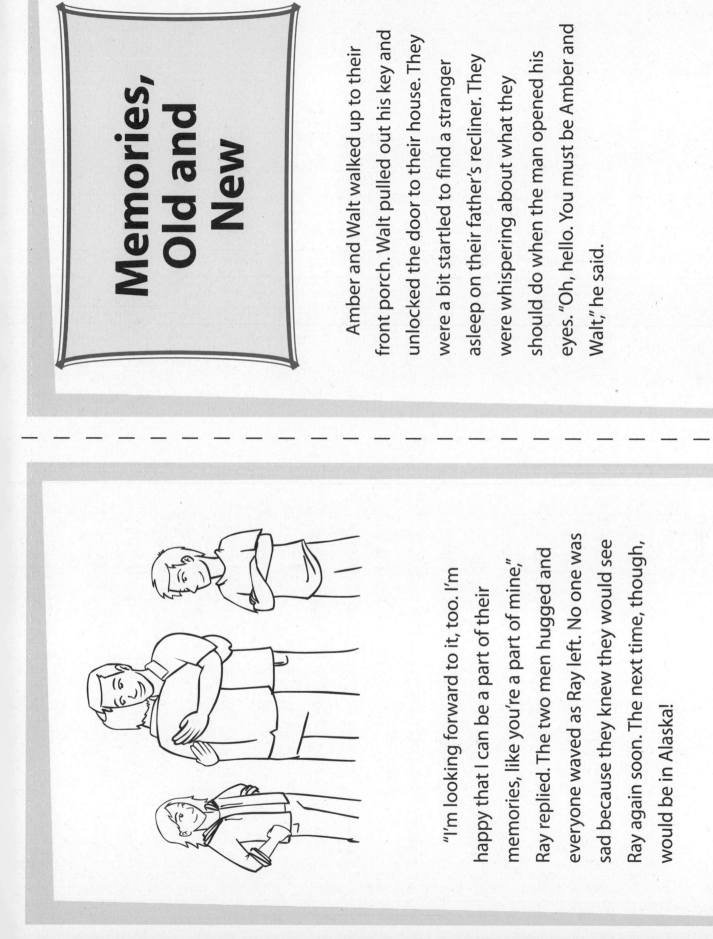

"I'm looking forward to it, too. I'm happy that I can be a part of their memories, like you're a part of mine," Ray replied. The two men hugged and everyone waved as Ray left. No one was sad because they knew they would see Ray again soon. The next time, though, would be in Alaska!

© 2009 K12 Inc. All rights reserved.

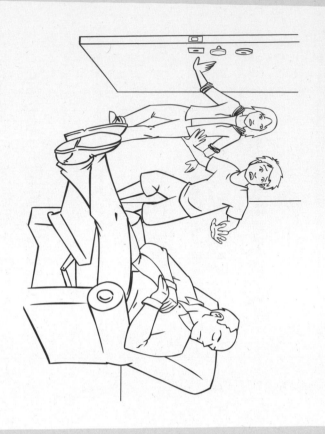

Amber and Walt weren't sure how to respond. They were uneasy with the fact that this stranger seemed to be so comfortable in their house, and that he knew their names. Before they could stammer out a reply, their father walked

© 2009 K12 Inc. All rights reserved.

© 2009 K12 Inc. All rights reserved.

"Well, I think you just got your answer," their father said to Ray. "It looks like we're coming to visit you in Alaska!"

Soon the room was buzzing with excitement. Amber and Walt listed everything they wanted to do on their trip. Their father and Ray talked about the best time to visit. By the end of the evening, everyone was looking forward to the trip.

"Well, I guess I should be going," Ray said. He stood up and walked to the front door. Amber, Walt, and their father walked with him.

"Thanks for inviting us to visit you, Ray," their father said. "As you can tell, we're all really looking forward to the trip."

into the room. "Hi, kids. I see you've met Mr. Brown," he said with excitement. "He's my oldest friend."

"Who are you calling old?" Mr. Brown replied. He and their father cackled with laughter at the joke. Then he turned to look at Amber and Walt. "Please, call me Ray," he said, extending his hand. Amber and Walt took turns shaking Ray's hand.

"It's nice to finally meet you," Amber said. "My dad has told us so many stories about you."

"Ray is visiting from Alaska. He came to town to visit his parents and he dropped by," their father explained. Without wasting any time, the two men began thinking back on some of their favorite memories. They talked

© 2009 K12 Inc. All rights reserved.

We even send text messages like you kids do. It's sad that we don't get to see each other very often, but we definitely keep in touch."

"That's part of the reason I came over here," Ray added. "Before you kids got home, I was talking to your father about you all taking a trip to come visit me in Alaska. There's plenty to see and do where I live. I think you'd all really enjoy it. What do you think?"

"I think that sounds like a great idea!" Amber shouted. "I'd like to see glaciers and Mt. McKinley."

"I'd love to go to Alaska!" Walt agreed. "I'd like to go rafting and ride a dog sled."

© 2009 K12 Inc. All rights reserved.

about their years in the drama club. They remembered ordering pizza and working on algebra. Amber and Walt had never seen their father laugh so hard. They couldn't help but laugh at some of the stories, too.

"Did your father ever tell you how we spent most of our free time growing up?" Ray asked. When Amber and Walt shook their heads, Ray continued. "We used to save up our allowance. Then on the weekends, we'd walk down to the arcade. See, back in those days, we didn't have all the video games you kids have now," Ray explained. "Anyway, we'd walk down to the arcade and spend hours feeding the machines quarters. Your dad and I got pretty good at

those games. One of us always held the records. It's too bad that arcade isn't around anymore. I'd like to challenge you to some of those games today!"

Everyone laughed at Ray's idea, but Walt seemed a little sad. "What's the matter, Walt?" his father asked.

"It's just kind of sad. You two have all these great memories from when you were growing up, but now you hardly ever talk," Walt explained. "Don't you miss each other?"

Ray and their father looked at each other with a confused expression. "I wouldn't say we hardly ever talk, Walt," his father replied. "With technology today, Ray and I communicate all the time. We talk on the phone. We e-mail.

© 2009 K12 Inc. All rights reserved.
© 2009 K12 Inc. All rights reserved.

Commonly Confused Words

Read each word and its definition. Choose the word that best completes each sentence below. Write that word on the line provided.

Word	Meaning
adapt	verb, to change one's self to reflect new circumstances
adopt	verb, to assume or accept
advice	noun, an opinion or suggestion given about a course of action or decision
advise	verb, to give information or notice, or to talk over a problem
affect	verb, to alter or change
effect	noun, a result

1. Paul listens well and considers all sides of an issue before giving any _____ .

2. The election results are in. The townspeople want to lower the speed limit. They will _____ a new law which will take effect immediately.

3. Since you want to spend time with your aunt, I am guessing her visit will _____ your work schedule quite a bit.

4. The cold medicine had no _____ on me. I still had a runny nose and a sore throat.

5. I know the kitten will _____ quickly to its new home if you are kind, gentle, and loving.

6. "I _____ you to eat your vegetables if you want to have dessert," my mother said.

© 2009 K12 Inc. All rights reserved.

Confusing Words and Root Word *dent*

Smile!

The root word *dent* means "tooth." Choose a word from the box to match each definition below. Write that word on the line provided.

dental   dentist   denture   dentistry

1. the profession of a dentist   _____

2. an adjective meaning "related to teeth"   _____

3. a person whose profession is the care of teeth   _____

4. a set of false teeth   _____

Choose two words from the box above. Write a sentence that uses each word on the lines provided below.

5. _____

_____

6. _____

_____

© 2009 K12 Inc. All rights reserved.

Get Ready

▪ **Compound Subjects:** When a sentence with one verb has two or more subjects, the sentence has a *compound subject*. Conjunctions join the subjects. In the following sentence, the two subjects are underlined, and the conjunction is in bold:

<u>Barb</u> **and** <u>I</u> will run in the annual 5K race this Sunday.

▪ **Compound Predicates:** When a sentence with one subject has two or more verbs, it has a *compound predicate*. Conjunctions join the verbs. In the following sentence, the verbs are underlined and the conjunction is in bold:

You can <u>walk</u> **or** <u>run</u> in the 5K race.

▪ Rather than having to write several, short sentences, the use of compound subjects and compound predicates allows us to write single, informative sentences.

Instead of: Bob is making chicken for the picnic. Mary is making chicken for the picnic. Sarah is making chicken for the picnic.

Compound subjects let us say: Bob, Mary, and Sarah are making chicken for the picnic.

Instead of: Dad made lunch. Dad went to the park.

Compound predicates let us say: Dad made lunch and went to the park.

© 2009 K12 Inc. All rights reserved.

Try It

In each sentence below, decide whether the sentence contains a compound subject or a compound predicate. Write "CS" on the line provided if the sentence has a compound subject. If the sentence has a compound predicate, write "CP" on the line provided. Then underline the compound subject or compound predicate in each sentence. The first one has been done for you as an example.

1. <u>Apples and pears</u> grow on this farm. __CP__

2. Are we eating at home or eating out tonight? _____

3. Jen and Beth study together. _____

4. I washed and dried my hands. _____

5. A singer or a dancer will lead the performance. _____

6. I laughed and cried at the movie last night. _____

7. Mom went shopping, did some cleaning, and cooked dinner today.

   _____

8. Bart and Kim had lunch at 1 p.m. _____

© 2009 K12 Inc. All rights reserved.

Commonly Confused Words

Use the definitions to unscramble the words in **bold**. Write each unscrambled word on the line provided.

1. _____ : **lseang** – guardians of human beings or people who are pure and lovely

2. _____ : **nasleg** – figures formed by two lines originating from the same point, or points of view

3. _____ : **necconiesc** – knowledge of right and wrong

4. _____ : **oncicosus** – intentional or deliberate, aware

5. _____ : **nceedt** – fairly good, such as in one's behavior, taste, or manners

6. _____ : **estdecn** – the act of going downward, or one's line of ancestors

Choose the word from each word pair above that correctly completes each sentence below. Write that word on the line provided.

7. We are studying right, acute, and obtuse _____ in math.

8. Ivan is _____ of the fact that his mother will be very upset if he is late getting home.

9. Your taste in clothing is not merely _____—it's incredible! Where did you find that beautiful dress?

© 2009 K12 Inc. All rights reserved.

The Root Word *meter*

The root word *meter* means "measure." Read each word and its definition.
Choose the word above that best completes each sentence below.
Write that word on the line provided.

Word	Meaning
diameter	the length of a straight line that passes through the center of an object from one side to the other
perimeter	the boundary or distance around a figure or area
speedometer	a device that shows the speed of a moving vehicle
barometer	an instrument that measures the pressure of the atmosphere, used especially in weather forecasting
pedometer	an instrument that measures the distance that someone walks

1. The rising _____ was an indication that good weather was coming our way.

2. We are going to put a fence around our garden's _____ to keep animals out.

3. Make sure you keep the _____ under 15 miles an hour here; there are many children in the area.

4. Half of a circle's _____ is called the circle's radius.

5. I used a _____ on my walk today and found out that I covered three miles in half an hour.

© 2009 K12 Inc. All rights reserved.

Clumsy No More

Kim was known for being clumsy. She had a habit of running into things. She was often picking herself up from a fall. She smashed her fingers and stubbed her toes all the time. Kim was careless, and she had the scrapes and bruises to prove it. Her mother always cautioned Kim to pay more attention. "Try to be careful, Kim. If you pay

© 2009 K12 Inc. All rights reserved.

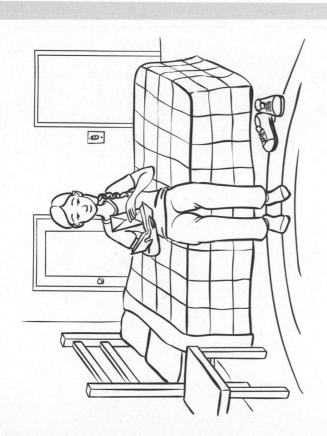

the details she could remember. At the end of the paper, she wrote the lesson she had learned: "Being careful brings great rewards." She folded the paper and placed it inside an envelope. From then on, Kim used that envelope as a bookmark, a reminder to always be careful.

© 2009 K12 Inc. All rights reserved.

© 2009 K12 Inc. All rights reserved.

attention to what you're doing, you won't have as many accidents," she advised. "You'll be safer and I won't have to worry about you as much."

Kim knew her mother was right. She hated being known as "Kim the Klutz."

© 2009 K12 Inc. All rights reserved.

Kim opened her eyes and stared up at the ceiling in her bedroom. "Wow, that was some dream," she said. She rolled out of her bed and patted her growling stomach. When she walked downstairs, her mother was waiting for her at the table.

During dinner, all Kim could talk about was her vivid dream of the Olympic games in ancient Greece. Her mother was especially impressed by Kim's new desire to be more careful. "Try to remember the lesson from your dream," she advised Kim.

After dinner, Kim walked back to her room. She was going to follow her mother's advice. Before she could forget her recent dream, Kim wrote down all of

The only way to get rid of that name was to be more careful. As she thought about her mother's advice, Kim drifted off into a nap. When she awoke, she didn't recognize her surroundings.

"Where am I?" Kim wondered aloud. She looked down at her clothing. "What am I wearing?" Her jeans and T-shirt had been replaced by a white cloth draped over one shoulder. Instead of the sneakers she had put on that morning, she was now wearing leather sandals. Kim looked around. The streets were different here. There were no paved roads or sidewalks. The people were different, too. They were all dressed in

© 2009 K12 Inc. All rights reserved.

© 2009 K12 Inc. All rights reserved.

As she watched each event, Kim was struck by how carefully the athletes hurled their disks, ran their races, and wrestled. "I see how important it is to be very cautious," Kim said. "Any small mistake in these games could be disastrous. One miscalculation, and they could be injured." Kim continued to watch the games in amazement. She couldn't believe that she was witnessing an event that she had only read about in books.

When the games ended, Kim began to follow the boy out of the stadium. She was hoping he would lead her to a place to eat because her stomach was growling. In the distance, she heard someone call her name. "Kim, dinner is ready."

the same white cloth and sandals that Kim was wearing. Kim was confused. She should have been in her bedroom. Instead, she was standing on the streets of a strange city, dressed in strange clothes. Kim realized that she was not only in a different place, she was also in a different time.

As she continued to look around, Kim noticed that everyone seemed to be going somewhere in a hurry. She decided to follow them. She turned to a boy walking beside her and tried to find some answers. "What's going on?" she asked.

"Why, everyone knows it's the Olympics," he replied.

© 2009 K12 Inc. All rights reserved.

"The Olympics?" Kim asked. "I've only watched those on television."

The boy looked at Kim with a confused expression. For a moment, she had forgotten she was in another time. She quickly realized that she was going to watch the Olympic games in ancient Greece!

Kim followed the little boy to the stadium. Once inside, they saw many athletes. Some athletes were preparing to hurl disks. Others were stretching before their races. In the distance, Kim spotted a pair of wrestlers. As the stadium filled with spectators, the excitement continued to grow. Just when Kim thought she couldn't wait any longer, the competition began.

© 2009 K12 Inc. All rights reserved.

Code Work

Confusing Words and Root Word *thermo*

Commonly Confused Words

Find and circle each word from the box in the word search chart below. Words may appear across, down, diagonally, or backward.

angel	pitcher	proceed	corporation
angle	envelop	precede	decent
picture	envelope	cooperation	descent

c	c	g	e	p	w	u	n	i	h	g	e	c	a
o	d	r	n	u	e	a	m	s	t	f	m	d	n
r	r	i	v	r	p	o	l	e	v	n	e	g	g
p	e	z	e	f	o	h	d	t	n	c	u	w	l
o	p	h	l	d	n	d	p	r	p	u	i	t	e
r	n	c	o	o	p	e	r	a	t	i	o	n	y
a	k	t	p	a	i	c	e	t	r	e	n	e	w
t	u	c	e	o	t	e	c	e	r	u	t	c	i
i	d	g	t	p	c	n	e	d	z	g	v	s	h
o	u	e	a	i	h	t	d	c	o	s	l	e	i
n	d	r	e	u	e	p	e	r	t	e	k	d	a
c	z	t	m	c	r	n	k	w	g	u	o	s	r
e	c	o	p	f	o	u	o	n	s	a	s	e	m
p	w	s	n	h	e	r	a	s	m	o	u	y	w
d	g	r	o	p	t	d	p	g	n	r	k	o	i

© 2009 K12 Inc. All rights reserved.

Confusing Words and Root Word *thermo*

The Root Word *thermo*

The root word *thermo* means "heat." Unscramble the words in **bold** below to match the given definitions. Write each word on the line provided.

Hint: Each word contains the root word *thermo*.

1. _____ : **ehmstro** – a container in which a vacuum between an inner and outer wall keeps liquids hot or cold

2. _____ : **mrehtetmore** – an instrument that measures temperature

3. _____ : **smhotatert** – a device that controls temperature

Choose the word from above that best completes each sentence below. Write that word on the line provided.

4. Whenever we leave the house during the winter, we set the _____ to 60 degrees so the cat and dog don't get too cold while we're away.

5. When Christina set out for the long drive, she filled a _____ with tea so that she could sip her favorite hot drink.

6. "Please place the _____ under your tongue so I can take your temperature," the nurse said.

© 2009 K12 Inc. All rights reserved.

Unit 11 Assessment

Part 1.

Underline the word in parentheses that best completes each sentence.

1. Having grown up in a big city, Carla found it hard to (adapt, adopt) to life on the small college campus.

2. Whenever I have a problem, I seek out my grandmother's wise (advice, advise).

3. Jose's drowsiness was an (affect, effect) of the medication he took.

4. "I need your full (corporation, cooperation) in this matter," the mayor said.

5. These photos are from my (recent, resent) trip to Alaska.

Part 2.

Underline the word in each word pair that matches each definition.

6. (angel, angle) – believed by some to be a guardian of human beings, or a person who is pure and lovely

7. (conscious, conscience) – knowledge of right and wrong

8. (envelop, envelope) – to surround or enclose

9. (proceed, precede) – to continue after a pause, or to move forward

10. (human, humane) – marked by consideration for others

© 2009 K12 Inc. All rights reserved.

Part 3.

Say each word aloud. Listen for the schwa sound /ə/. On the line provided, write the number of times the schwa sound /ə/ is heard in each word.

Hint: Not all words below contain the schwa sound /ə/.

11. banana _____

12. aware _____

13. arena _____

14. agreeable _____

15. data _____

16. drama _____

17. apple _____

18. comfortable _____

19. abbreviation _____

20. after _____

Part 4.

Underline the words in the box below that contain the schwa sound /ə/.

21.

pizza	chair	apply	pasta	ask
farm	assume	cinema	apologize	ago
aroma	alarm	candle	scuba	spray

© 2009 K12 Inc. All rights reserved.

Part 5.

Read the paragraphs below. Underline the words that contain the schwa sound /ə/.

22. I am swimming peacefully in calm aqua waters. I love to scuba dive. Schools of fish are all around me. One fish draws my attention. It is bright orange with specks of black. It is not aware that I'm there, so I can get very close to it—almost close enough to touch.

I suddenly get a strange feeling. I am afraid, but I don't know why. It is as if I am being watched. I start to swim to the surface when I see it. A shark, about twenty feet away, appears out of nowhere. I freeze in fright.

Buzzz! My alarm goes off. I am alone in my room. Thank goodness! It was just a dream.

Part 6.

Listen to each word as it is read to you. Write each word on the line provided below.

23. _____

24. _____

25. _____

26. _____

27. _____

28. _____

© 2009 K12 Inc. All rights reserved.

Part 7.
Draw a line to connect each root word at left to its meaning on the right.

29.	brev	heat
30.	tech	tooth
31.	thermo	short
32.	dent	art or skill
33.	tox	measure
34.	meter	poison

Part 8.
Circle the word that best completes each sentence below.

35. The day care center staff makes sure that none of their art supplies are _____.

(toxic, thermos, perimeter)

36. When my sister was learning to drive, my mother liked to crane her neck to see what the _____ read.

(diameter, thermometer, speedometer)

37. Inc. is the _____ for the word incorporated.

(denture, toxicology, abbreviation)

38. I asked the body shop repairman to be a little less _____ in his explanation of what was wrong with my car. I couldn't understand half of what he was saying.

(technical, kilometer, abbreviated)

© 2009 K12 Inc. All rights reserved.

Who's Who

Rewrite each of the following titles by using abbreviations.
Hint: If an abbreviation is used in the name of a specific business or organization, the first letter of that abbreviation is capitalized.

1. Mary Jones, assistant director

_____

2. The Bee Tree, Incorporated

_____

3. Carson City Firehouse Number 5

_____

4. James Chan, president of student government

_____

5. The Southside Company

_____

6. Harold Jackson, government inspector

_____

7. Margaret Scott, president

_____

8. Steve Green, company assistant

_____

9. Anna Gonzales, company president

_____

© 2009 K12 Inc. All rights reserved.

Using the Root Word *bell*

The root word *bell* means "war, or to fight." Choose a word from the box to match each word or phrase below. Write each word on the line provided and read each word aloud.

Hint: One word will be used twice.

belligerent	rebel	rebellion

1. the act of fighting back, defiance, or disobedience   _____

2. to fight back or struggle against any kind of control   _____

3. person, group, or nation that shows a readiness to fight or wage war   _____

4. one who fights back against any kind of control or authority   _____

Choose a word from the box above to complete each sentence below. Write that word on the line provided. Then read each sentence aloud.
Hint: One word will be used twice.

5. The _____ who destroyed the buildings was sent to prison.

6. The _____ began after the king unfairly taxed the people.

7. The group was _____ after the governor proposed higher taxes.

8. The group of workers made plans to _____ if their manager did not listen to their concerns.

© 2009 K12 Inc. All rights reserved.

Get Ready

A compound direct object is two or more direct objects, connected by a conjunction. The direct object answers the questions *whom* or *what* after the action verb.

I will call **Jen or Beth** and ask directions.

Whom did I call? Jen, Beth. The conjunction *or* lets us connect the two direct objects.

I bought **shirts and shoe**s at the mall.

What did I buy? Shirts, shoes. The conjunction *and* lets us connect the two direct objects.

© 2009 K12 Inc. All rights reserved.

Try It

Write five sentences on the lines provided below. In each sentence, be sure to use a compound direct object.

1. _____

_____

2. _____

_____

3. _____

_____

4. _____

_____

5. _____

_____

© 2009 K12 Inc. All rights reserved.

Abbreviations

On the lines provided, rewrite each of the following units of measurement by using abbreviations.

1. ounce _____

2. pint _____

3. pound _____

4. quart _____

5. square _____

Complete the shopping list below. On the line provided, write the abbreviation for the unit of measurement written below that line.

Shopping List

1 _____ milk
   quart

1 _____ potatoes
   pound

1 _____ orange juice
   pint

1 eight-_____ bottle of vegetable oil
   ounce

© 2009 K12 Inc. All rights reserved.

Using the Root Word *just*

The root word *just* means "law." Choose a word from the box to match each word or phrase. Write each word on the line provided, and then read each word aloud.

injustice	just	justice	justify	unjust

1. adjective meaning "fair or lawful" _____

2. noun meaning "fair or lawful treatment" _____

3. verb meaning "to show to be right, or to give good reasons for" _____

4. adjective meaning "not fair or lawful" _____

5. noun meaning "not fair or lawful treatment" _____

Choose the word from the box above that best completes each sentence below. Write each word on the line provided. Then read each sentence aloud.

6. It was difficult to _____ the expensive price of the bicycle.

7. The innocent man was shown _____ when the jury declared him not guilty.

8. America's judicial system is based on _____ laws.

9. The volunteer group works to prevent _____ worldwide.

10. A large group of people protested the _____ actions of the local business owners.

© 2009 K12 Inc. All rights reserved.

Last-Minute Assistant

"I'm never going to be able to get everything done in time," Chang complained to Trey over the phone. "I really regret volunteering to host the debate club dinner tonight. I thought it was going to be fun, but now it's turned out to be more work than I can handle."

"Don't beat yourself up, Chang. When you volunteered, you didn't realize you were going to have such a crazy week,"

© 2009 K12 Inc. All rights reserved.

When the guests arrived, everyone was impressed. The house looked great and the food smelled delicious. They complimented Chang on his hard work. He thanked them, but he made sure to give Trey credit, too. "I couldn't have done it without my assistant," Chang said, pointing to Trey.

Trey smiled and gave Chang a high five. "That's what friends are for," he replied. "Just keep this day in mind the next time I need an assistant!"

Trey pointed out. "How could you know that your swim team was going to make it to the championships and you would have to practice every night this week?"

"You're right, but that excuse really doesn't help me. I still need to decorate the house and make dinner for 10 people, and I have to do it all within a few hours," Chang sighed. "I'm sorry to cut this phone call short, Trey, but I really need to get started. I haven't even been to the grocery store to buy the ingredients for dinner!"

Minutes after Chang and Trey said their good-byes, Chang heard a knock at his door. He opened it to find Trey standing on the other side. "Help has

© 2009 K12 Inc. All rights reserved.

quite silly running around the house and the grocery store with their panicked expressions. Thinking about the scene while they cooked dinner was enough to send them into fits of laughter.

© 2009 K12 Inc. All rights reserved.

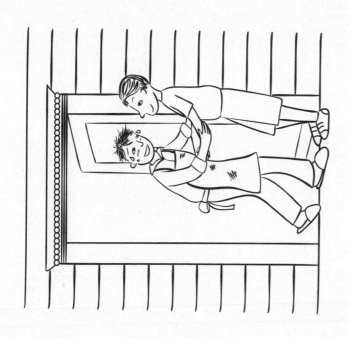

arrived!" Trey shouted as he stepped inside. "You have a lot to do, and not much time to do it. I'm here to help you get it all done."

© 2009 K12 Inc. All rights reserved.

---

around the kitchen and bumped into each more times than they could count. One messy hour later, all of the food was prepared, the kitchen was clean, and the house was completely decorated.

Chang sat down and let out a long sigh. "Thank you so much, Trey. I know I wouldn't have been able to pull off this dinner without you," he said to his friend. "We even have a few minutes to catch our breath before the guests arrive."

"'I'm glad I could help," Trey replied. "I know everyone is going to have a great time tonight. No one ever has to know it almost didn't happen!"The two boys relaxed and looked back on their day. They thought they must have looked

© 2009 K12 Inc. All rights reserved.

© 2009 K12 Inc. All rights reserved.

"You're the best, Trey!" Chang replied.

"How do you feel about going to the grocery store for me? I can stay home and decorate the house while you're gone. Then when you come back, we can cook the food. With your help, I think everything will be ready for the debate club later tonight!" Trey could hear the relief in Chang's voice.

After Trey grabbed a pen and paper, Chang started rattling off his grocery list. "We need a pound of potatoes, a pint of milk, and a quart of chocolate ice cream. We also need a pound of tomatoes, a pint of strawberries, and half a pound of cherries. I have everything else," Chang said.

© 2009 K12 Inc. All rights reserved.

"Can you repeat the second half of your list? You were talking so fast, I couldn't keep up," Trey said.

Chang glanced at the list Trey had made. "That's because you're writing out the entire words," Chang observed. "Just use the abbreviations. You'll be able to write faster, which means you can get to the grocery store sooner!"

Trey slapped his forehead with his hand. "Of course! I should be using the abbreviations," he said. "Why didn't I think of that?" Trey finished the grocery list and left Chang to decorate. When Trey returned with the groceries, he helped Chang make dinner. The two scrambled

Part 5.

Read the sentences below. Underline *true* if the rule is correct; underline *false* if the rule is incorrect.

21. An abbreviation is a shortened form of a word or phrase.
    (true, false)

22. If an abbreviation is used in the name of a specific business or organization, the first letter of the abbreviation is capitalized.
    (true, false)

23. An abbreviation always ends with a period.
    (true, false)

Part 6.

Read each definition below. Choose the correct root word from the second line to match each definition. Write that word on the line provided.

24. Definition: war or to fight
    Root words: bell, ini, just

    Answer: _____

25. Definition: law
    Root words: bell, ini, just

    Answer: _____

26. Definition: beginning
    Root words: bell, ini, just

    Answer: _____

© 2009 K12 Inc. All rights reserved.

Part 7.

Read each definition below. Choose the correct word from the second line to match each definition, and write that word on the line provided.

27. Definition: fair or lawful treatment

Words: initial, initiative, justice, justify, rebel, rebellion

Answer: _____

28. Definition: the act of fighting back or disobedience

Words: initial, initiative, justice, justify, rebel, rebellion

Answer: _____

29. Definition: the ability to get things started without being told what to do

Words: initial, initiative, justice, justify, rebel, rebellion

Answer: _____

Part 8.

Choose the word from the box that best completes each sentence below.
Write that word on the line provided.

belligerent	initial	initiate	just	rebel	unjust

30. Juan's _____ reaction to the news was one of shock.

31. The _____ group protested the rise in prices.

32. The newspaper reported the _____ actions of the president against his country's citizens.

© 2009 K12 Inc. All rights reserved.

Get Ready

- Pretend you are standing on the beach, watching the ocean. If you were to describe the waves, maybe you would say:

    The waves crash loudly on the shore.

    This sentence has *natural order*. In a sentence with natural order, the subject (*waves*) comes before the verb (*crash*).

- But if you were writing a poem or a story, you might want to add some style to the sentence. Instead, you might say:

    Loudly crash the waves on the shore.

    This is called *inverted order*. A sentence with inverted order has a verb or a helping verb before the subject.

- Inverted order is common in questions. Questions usually include divided verb phrases, the helping verb coming before the subject and the main verb coming after the subject.

    Do the waves crash loudly on the shore?

    The subject is *waves*, but the helping verb, *do* comes before the subject, so the sentence has inverted order.

© 2009 K12 Inc. All rights reserved.

Try It

On the lines provided after each sentence, write "N" if the sentence has natural order or write "I" if the sentence has inverted order.

1. In her ear buzzed a mosquito. _____

2. He needs to use the sewing machine today. _____

3. Can you see the mountain from here? _____

4. When will the rock concert begin? _____

5. Long ago lived a queen in a castle. _____

6. Jimmy is mowing the lawn because Dad broke his foot. _____

7. The old green canoe slapped against the dock. _____

8. Out from under the porch crawled a very dirty Bobby. _____

On the lines provided, write a sentence with natural order. Then, rewrite the sentence with inverted order.

9. Natural order: _____

   _____

10. Inverted order: _____

   _____

© 2009 K12 Inc. All rights reserved.

Related Words

Choose the word from the box that matches each clue below. Write each word on the line provided. Read aloud each word that you write.

atom	janitor	major	perspire
atomic	janitorial	majority	perspiration

1. one of the smallest parts of matter _____

2. more than half _____

3. to sweat _____

4. related to cleaning services _____

Choose the word from the box above that best completes each sentence below. Write each word on the line provided. Then read each sentence aloud.

5. Nuclear energy is the same as _____ energy.

6. My shirt was wet with _____ after I ran the race.

7. The scientist made a _____ discovery while researching the animals.

8. The _____ at my mother's office cleans every night while the office is closed.

© 2009 K12 Inc. All rights reserved.

Using the Root Word *liber*

The root word *liber* means "free." Choose the word from the box that matches each definition below. Write that word on the line provided. Then read each word aloud.

Hint: One word will be used more than once.

liberal	liberate	liberty

1. to set free _____

2. open to new ideas _____

3. generous or given freely _____

4. the condition of being free from _____
   the control of others

Choose the word from the box above that best completes each sentence below. Write each word on the line provided. Then read each sentence aloud.

Hint: One word will be used more than once.

5. The organization gave a _____ donation to the charity group.

6. The colonists fought for _____ in the Revolutionary War.

7. My parents have a more _____ way of thinking than my grandparents.

8. In the story, the woman fought hard to _____ herself from her captors.

© 2009 K12 Inc. All rights reserved.

Atomic Ant

"John, will you tell me the Atomic Ant story?" Kelsey asked as she kicked off her slippers and slid under the covers. "It's my favorite bedtime story."

"I know it's your favorite. I've told it to you a million times. I used to have to read it from the book, but now I have it memorized," he replied. "I'll tell you the story one time, but then you have to go to bed," he said. John sat down beside Kelsey and began the story.

© 2009 K12 Inc. All rights reserved.

---

generous and thoughtful gifts. It was then that he realized that he liked living with other animals. Life was more fun and interesting when he had friends to share everything with. From then on, Atomic Ant gladly spent his days with his friends in the forest."

John finished the story and looked at his sister. He expected to find her asleep. Instead, she was looking at the ceiling and smiling. "I agree with Atomic Ant," she said. "Life is better with friends and family. After all, who else is going to tell you your favorite bedtime story every night?" She turned to her brother and gave him a big hug. Although he didn't say it, John agreed with Atomic Ant, too.

© 2009 K12 Inc. All rights reserved.

"This is the story of Atomic Ant. Like all ants, Atomic Ant was tiny. That, however, is where the similarities stopped. Atomic Ant was smarter and mightier than all other ants, and he preferred to live alone instead of in a colony. His mission in life

© 2009 K12 Inc. All rights reserved.

beak from a tree trunk. Atomic Ant rushed to the scene. He ran up the tree trunk to get a closer look at the wife's stuck beak. Then he came up with a plan. Atomic Ant used his tiny fists and his great strength to carefully chip the wood around her beak. After a few minutes of Ant's punching the tree, the woodpecker was free. She thanked Atomic Ant for rescuing her from a dangerous situation.

"Stories of Atomic Ant's great deeds traveled throughout the forest. All the forest animals agreed that Atomic Ant deserved to be recognized for all his heroic acts. The animals made him a special suit out of silk and a helmet out of stone. Atomic Ant was touched by the

© 2009 K12 Inc. All rights reserved.

was to help animals that were in danger, and he couldn't do that if he lived as other ants did.

"One day, Atomic Ant was exercising. First he lifted weights. Then he went for a run through the forest. It was on this run that he came across an injured bear. The bear's paw was caught in a trap, and he was in pain. He was drenched with perspiration from all of his struggling to break free of the trap. Atomic Ant looked at the bear and knew that he had to help. He rushed to the bear's aid, only to be greeted with a snort of disbelief. The bear looked down at the tiny ant and shook his head. Atomic Ant tried to convince the bear that he was there to help, but the bear couldn't imagine how a tiny ant was going to free him from

© 2009 K12 Inc. All rights reserved.

"Atomic Ant was not used to all of this attention. He was used to living alone, without any attention from anyone. Suddenly his life had changed. Night and day, countless animals would knock on his door and ask him for help. One time, a deer asked him to find his son who was lost. Atomic Ant ran through the forest looking for the lost deer. Soon he spotted him, trapped behind some boulders that had fallen and blocked the path. Atomic Ant wasted no time. He threw the boulders out of the way and led the deer back to his father. Both deer thanked Atomic Ant for his help.

"Another time, a woodpecker asked Atomic Ant to help his wife free her

© 2009 K12 Inc. All rights reserved.

© 2009 K12 Inc. All rights reserved.

such a large trap. The bear had spent all day trying to free himself, but he had been unsuccessful. Surely this tiny ant would also fail.

"Undiscouraged, Atomic Ant rushed to the bear's trapped paw to take a closer look. He quickly came up with

© 2009 K12 Inc. All rights reserved.

a plan. He was going to use his small size to his advantage. He planned to wiggle into the lock of the trap. Then he would pull the lock's latch and free the bear. Within seconds, Atomic Ant had liberated the bear from the painful trap. The huge bear looked down at the little ant and thanked him. He apologized to Atomic Ant for thinking he was too tiny to be of any use. That day, the bear realized that even the tiniest of creatures are able to do great things.

"News quickly spread through the forest about a tiny ant saving the big bear. Soon, Atomic Ant became a hero among the other forest animals. They all wanted to meet the brave and mighty ant.

Code Work

Name:

Word Relationships and Root Word *cline*

Related Words

Use the clues to fill in the words in the crossword. The first one has been done for you.

Across

1. to hold a position of authority or to be in charge
2. the act of giving up a position
3. to put something back into its original state or condition

Down

3. to give up a position
4. the act of putting something back into its original state or condition
5. a person elected to have authority

© 2009 K12 Inc. All rights reserved.

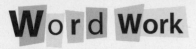
Using the Root Word *cline*

The root word *cline* means "to lean." Choose the word from the box that matches each phrase below. Write that word on the line provided. Then read each word aloud.

Hint: Two words will be used more than once.

decline	incline	recline

1. to lean, slope, or slant _____

2. to lie down or to lean back _____

3. to slope or lean downward _____

4. a sloping or leaning surface _____

5. a weakening in health, power, or value _____

Choose the word from the box above that best completes each sentence below. Write that word on the line provided. Then read each sentence aloud.

6. I like to _____ on the porch swing and read a good book.

7. Recently, there has been a _____ in the price of computers.

8. We drove up a sharp _____ to the lake and campgrounds.

© 2009 K12 Inc. All rights reserved.

Related Words

Choose the word from the box that matches each clue below. Write that word on the line provided. Read aloud each word that you write.

advantageous	angelic	musical

1. description of very good behavior _____

2. related to music _____

3. favorable _____

Use each word from the box above to help you spell a related word that will complete one of the sentences below. Write the related form of that word on the line provided. Then read each sentence aloud.

4. We used our knowledge of the mountains to our _____ during the hike.

5. The artist worked for months on the painting of the _____ .

6. My sister is a talented _____ who plays the piano, flute, and guitar.

© 2009 K12 Inc. All rights reserved.

Using the Root Word *cert*

The root word *cert* means "sure or definite." Choose the word from the box that matches each definition below. Write that word on the line provided. Then read each word aloud.

certain	certificate	certify

1. sure or without doubt   _____

2. a written statement that is proof   _____
   of a particular fact

3. to indicate the truth of a fact in   _____
   a written document; to confirm,
   to verify

Choose the word from the box above that best completes each sentence below. Write that word on the line provided. Then read each sentence aloud.

4. The team doctor will _____ the health of the players.

5. The lawyer must be _____ about the facts of the case.

6. Mom framed the _____ and hung it in the living room.

© 2009 K12 Inc. All rights reserved.

sic
...ories
...eams

...final items to
...her parents
...ave for their trip to
...een looking forward
...ths. Now that the
...rived, she felt as if she
...inute longer. "Hurry,
...ll be here soon," her
...That was all Eve needed
...With her luggage in one hand
...d her violin in the other, she raced
downstairs.

Eve neve...
She never
sounded o...
it was that...
mind many years...
another dream. Eve was...
her first day of work as a r...
Now she could use her vio...
musical talent to help othe...
their own dreams.

© 2009 K12 Inc. All rights reserved.

© 2009 K12 Inc. All rights reserved.

Eve and her parents loaded everything into the taxi and headed for the airport. During the ride, Eve couldn't stop talking about their trip. She told the taxi driver about all of their plans for their time in Chicago. She asked her parents a long list of questions, all of which she'd asked in the past. It was obvious that Eve was excited about this trip.

Once at the airport, Eve and her parents checked in and walked to their gate. While they waited for their flight, Eve opened her violin case. The elegant case and violin that lay within had been a present from her parents years ago. They had it custom-made for Eve from the finest wood. They even had her name engraved on the back. It was her most treasured possession.

© 2009 K12 Inc. All rights reserved.

Once inside, Eve's parents handed the usher their tickets and he led them to their seats. Eve could not sit still as they waited for the performance to begin. Her excitement grew as the seats began to fill up. Soon the lights turned off. After waiting for what felt like hours, Eve saw Haley Rubin take the stage. Eve held her breath. She watched as Haley pulled her violin up to her chin, just as Eve had done so many times herself. Haley's music started out soft and slow, and then quickly built to loud and fast. Throughout the performance, Eve never took her eyes off the talented musician. Eve was amazed at what she saw and felt. The melodies that flowed from Haley's violin moved Eve. It was as if Eve could feel the music in her heart.

© 2009 K12 Inc. All rights reserved.

GATE
108

As Eve looked at her violin, she thought back to the first day she played it. She remembered it like it was yesterday. Eve didn't know it at the time, but that day was the beginning of something special for her. Eve

© 2009 K12 Inc. All rights reserved.

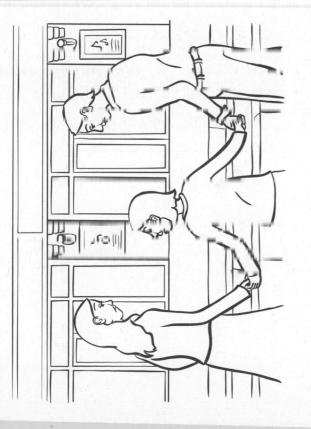

were no dinner reservations. Her parents were making her dream come true! Tears began to well in Eve's eyes and she embraced her parents tightly. This was the best surprise of her life! Eve smiled at her parents and reached for their hands. Together they entered the performance hall.

© 2009 K12 Inc. All rights reserved.

remembered how the violin fit perfectly between her shoulder and chin. She remembered how comfortable the bow felt in her hand. Without any instruction, her fingers seemed to know their place on the strings. From her first note, everyone agreed that Eve was a natural. Through the years, she had collected enough trophies and ribbons from musical competitions to prove them right.

Eve closed her violin case. "I can't believe we're going to be in Chicago at the same time as Haley Rubin. She's my favorite violinist," she said to her parents. "I listen to her music all of the time. I've even learned to play some of her songs. It's too bad her concert is sold out. I would have loved to see her perform."

"We know seeing her perform is a dream of yours. Perhaps that dream will come true for you someday," her mother replied, as they boarded the plane.

Soon Eve and her parents were in their hotel room in Chicago. When it was time for dinner, her father looked at Eve. "Are you ready? We have dinner reservations and we don't want to be late," he said. They left their hotel and boarded a taxi. After a short ride, they stepped out of the car. It took Eve a second to realize the building she was standing in front of was not a restaurant. It was too big to be a restaurant. Eve quickly grasped where she stood. She recognized the building from books and magazines she had read. It was Chicago's finest performance hall. It suddenly dawned on her that there

All rights reserved.

Related Words

Use the clues to fill in the words in the crossword. The first one has been done for you.

Across

1. a doctor of medicine
3. sight, hearing, smell, touch, or taste
5. an explosive device

Down

2. an examination of the body or a checkup
4. reasonable
6. to continue directing questions or requests

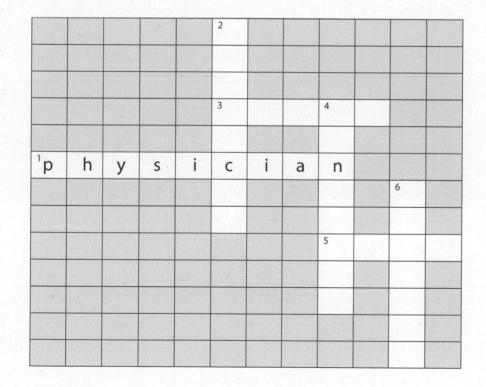

© 2009 K12 Inc. All rights reserved.

Using the Root Word *astro*

The root word *astro* means "star." Choose the word from the box that matches each phrase below. Write that word on the line provided. Then read each word aloud.

astronaut astronomer astronomy

1. a traveler in space _____

2. the study of the stars and other heavenly bodies _____

3. one who studies the stars and other heavenly bodies _____

Choose the word from the box above that best completes each sentence below. Write that word on the line provided. Then read each sentence aloud.

4. The _____ calculated the distance to the star.

5. Stars, planets, meteors, and asteroids are all studied in _____ .

6. The _____ must complete her training before she can go on the space mission.

© 2009 K12 Inc. All rights reserved.

Get Ready

■ There are four types of sentences.

Sentences that make a statement are called *declarative sentences*. Declarative sentences end with a period.

It's a cool day today.

■ Sentences that ask a question are called *interrogative sentences*. Interrogative sentences end with a question mark.

Do you think I'll need a coat?

■ Sentences that give a command are called *imperative sentences*. Imperative sentences end with a period.

Put your sweater on.

■ Sentences that express strong emotion are called *exclamatory sentences*. Exclamatory sentences end with an exclamation point.

What a beautiful day!

■ **Remember:**
Declarative sentences make a statement.
Interrogative sentences ask a question.
Imperative sentences give a command.
Exclamatory sentences express strong emotion.

© 2009 K12 Inc. All rights reserved.

Try It

Draw a line to match the sentence type on the left to the correct example sentence on the right.

Declarative   Buy the tickets online.

Interrogative   I would like to go to the movies today

Imperative   I can't wait to go!

Exclamatory   What time are you going to the movies?

For each sentence type, write one sentence on the lines provided below. Remember to use the proper punctuation for each sentence type.

Declarative: _____

_____

Interrogative: _____

_____

Imperative: _____

_____

Exclamatory: _____

_____

© 2009 K12 Inc. All rights reserved.

Code Work

Word Relationships and Root Word *domus*

Related Words

Choose the word from the box that matches each clue below. Write that word on the line provided. Read aloud each word that you write.

| define   opposite   personality   practical |

1. useful   _____

2. explain   _____

3. as different as possible   _____

4. the traits of a person's character   _____

Use each word from the box above to help spell a related word that will complete one of the sentences below. Write the related form of that word on the line provided. Then read each sentence aloud.

5. I _____ playing the piano every day.

6. My sister and I always share our _____ thoughts.

7. There is a _____ date set for the trip to the Grand Canyon.

8. He did not _____ my idea to divide the work equally between the two of us.

© 2009 K12 Inc. All rights reserved.

Using the Root Word *domus*

The root word *domus* means "house." Choose the word from the box that matches each phrase below. Write that word on the line provided. Then read each word aloud.

domestic   domesticate   domicile

1. a person's home   _____

2. having to do with home or family   _____

3. to train to live with, and be made   _____
     useful to, humans

Choose the word from the box above that best completes each sentence below. Write that word on the line provided. Then read each sentence aloud.

4. Dogs are _____ animals today, but long ago they were wild.

5. Do you think people will ever try to _____ wild animals such as lions and tigers?

6. Most people call the place where they live their home, instead of their _____ .

© 2009 K12 Inc. All rights reserved.

The Fountain of Wisdom

Mr. Ramsey looked at his watch. It was already 6:30 in the evening. *Where is she?* he wondered to himself, as he looked out the glass door of the building. He set down his briefcase, then sat down in one of the cushioned leather chairs in the lobby. He closed his eyes and let out a big sigh. The sound of the nearby water fountain helped him calm down. He reclined deeper into the chair. The sound of the water reminded

© 2009 K12 Inc. All rights reserved.

---

car weren't in the shop, and if your wife hadn't been late, we never would have had this lovely chat." Mr. Ito gave Mr. Ramsey a sincere smile. He got up and began to push his cleaning cart down the hallway. "Remember, Mr. Ramsey, it's just as easy to look for the good as it is for the bad." With that, he was gone.

Just then, Mr. Ramsey heard a horn honk outside the door. H⎯⎯⎯ ⎯⎯ outside and jumped into the car. As ⎯⎯ ⎯⎯⎯⎯led into his seat, he said, "I had the most interesting conversation just now. That Mr. Ito—what an odd personality." Mr. Ramsey was quiet for several minutes. Then suddenly, he said, "I'll tell you one thing, Alice. I will never judge another person by what they do for a living." His wife looked puzzled. "And remind me to call my mom when we get home. I need to say 'thanks.'"

© 2009 K12 Inc. All rights reserved.

© 2009 K12 Inc. All rights reserved.

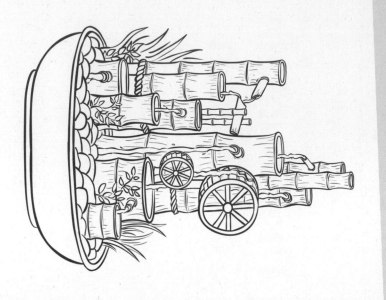

him of a babbling brook. Mr. Ramsey started to think about his secret fishing spot back where he grew up.

Several minutes passed before Mr. Ramsey realized someone was in the lobby with him. He opened his eyes with

---

© 2009 K12 Inc. All rights reserved.

I have the chance to return the favor. And it's turned out to be a blessing. I'm getting to know her all over again. We have wonderful talks during the day, and she's teaching me how to make some of my favorite childhood foods. I couldn't be happier!" he said. "I learned how to make fresh Japanese noodles just this afternoon. What a treat!" he said, chuckling.

"That's a great way of looking at things," replied Mr. Ramsey.

"My father taught me to look for the good in everything," Mr. Ito said, as he sat down beside Mr. Ramsey. "It's like you and your car. You probably think it was a bad thing for it to break down. And now your wife is late picking you up. That probably added to your bad mood. But I see it as a good thing. If your a start and saw Mr. Ito polishing the brass railing near the stairway. "Oh, hello, Mr. Ito!" Mr. Ramsey said as he sat up. "I didn't know you were working in here."

"Nice to see you, Mr. Ramsey," replied Mr. Ito. "Is everything OK? It's unusual to see you here so late, and in the lobby, at that."

"My car is in the shop," Mr. Ramsey sighed. "My wife was supposed to pick me up an hour ago. She must be stuck in a meeting at work. I thought I'd sit here in the lobby instead of my office. It's kind of relaxing here, with all the plants. And I love listening to that water fountain," he said, pointing to the fountain near the door. "The sound of the trickling water is so soothing. Today I need to be soothed!"

© 2009 K12 Inc. All rights reserved.

up his job to take care of someone, even his mother. "I'm not sure I could make such a personal sacrifice."

"Actually, it was just the opposite. I didn't give it a second thought," Mr. Ito replied casually. "She's my mother. She took care of me when I was a child. Now

© 2009 K¯2 Inc. All rights reserved.

"I'm sorry you're having car trouble," said Mr. Ito, "but I'm pleased to hear that you like the fountain. I built that fountain from scratch. And that's exactly why I put it in here. And I thought it was a good way to begin and end the workday." He walked over to the fountain and added some fresh water to the top bowl. He pulled a cloth from his pocket and gave it a quick dusting.

"You made that fountain?" Mr. Ramsey asked, in disbelief. He found it hard to believe. *After all, he's only a janitor,* he thought to himself.

"Yes, I used to have a job as a mechanical engineer," Mr. Ito said in a matter-of-fact way. "But I still like to put things together in my workshop at home. I build all sorts of mechanical things. It's good practice."

© 2009 K12 Inc. All rights reserved.

"You were a mechanical engineer?" Mr. Ramsey asked, again in disbelief. "If you don't mind my asking, how did you end up here on the janitorial staff?" Mr. Ramsey was definitely interested in Mr. Ito's story.

"Well, my mother is getting older," Mr. Ito explained. "She can't live by herself anymore. So my wife and I asked her to move in with us. Mother can't be left alone—it's not safe. Both my wife and I had day jobs, so I decided to quit mine and take this night job. That way I could look after Mother during the day. My wife takes care of her at night, while I'm here at work," he said. "It's quite a practical arrangement."

"That must have been a hard decision to make," said Mr. Ramsey. He was thinking of how he would hate giving

© 2009 K12 Inc. All rights reserved.

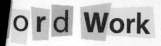
Using the Root Word *min*

The root word *min* means "small." Choose the word from the box that matches each word or phrase below. Write that word on the line provided. Then read each word aloud.

miniature   minimum   minus

1. without, or not having _____

2. small _____

3. smallest amount or number that _____
   is possible or allowed

Choose the word from the box above that best completes each sentence below. Write each word on the lines provided. Then read each sentence aloud.

4. In the heavy rain, I felt sorry for the man who was

   _____ an umbrella.

5. The _____ poodle took first prize in the small-
   dog contest.

6. Fifty dollars is the _____ amount that I will
   accept for the bike I'm selling.

© 2009 K12 Inc. All rights reserved.

Related Words

Use the clues to fill in the words in the crossword. The first one has been done for you.

Across

1. an object, mark, or sign that stands for something else

2. not hard or firm

4. connected

Down

1. to make less hard or less firm

3. related to an object, mark, or sign that stands for something else

4. a person in the same family by blood or marriage

© 2009 K12 Inc. All rights reserved.

Word Relationships and Root Word *mand*

Root Word Practice

Underline each word in the chart that has a meaning related to "orders."

incline	domestic	astronaut	uncertain	demand
mandatory	justice	decline	belligerent	certify
rebellion	initial	thermos	just	abbreviate
thermometer	mandate	astronomy	liberation	recline
initiative	liberate	command	domicile	thermostat

Choose three of the words that you underlined above. On the lines provided below, write a sentence that uses each word.

1. _____

_____

2. _____

_____

3. _____

_____

© 2009 K12 Inc. All rights reserved.

Word Relationships and Root Word *min*

Related Words

Choose the word from the box that matches each clue below. Write that word on the line provided. Read aloud each word that you write.

population	public	signature

1. people located or gathered in an area _____

2. a person's name written by that person _____

3. all the people living in a particular city, country, or other area _____

Use each word from the box above to help spell a related word that will complete one of the sentences below. Write the related form of that word on the line provided. Then read each sentence aloud.

4. Skiing and snowboarding are _____ activities during winter.

5. The group held a press conference to gain _____ for their cause.

6. I asked my mother to _____ the permission slip allowing me to attend soccer camp.

© 2009 K12 Inc. All rights reserved.

The Tyler Jenkins Library

"Can you believe it?" Tyler shouted to his family as he entered the dining room. "After all this time, we finally have our public library back! I can't wait to see how they've fixed it up." Tyler grabbed a plate and sat down at the breakfast table.

"I remember how you walked all over town, collecting signatures for that petition of yours," said Dad. "You sure were a determined young man."

© 2009 K12 Inc. All rights reserved.

"I don't think so, Tyler," said Mom. "It's one of those things people mean to do, but they never get around to actually doing it. I think what you did is really outstanding. You should take credit for all your efforts."

"Okay, everybody! Let's get dressed and head over to the new library," said Karen as she placed her sticky plate in the sink. "Oh, excuse me. Make that the Tyler Jenkins Library!" she said in an angelic voice. Tyler blushed again. But secretly, he wished it were true!

© 2009 K12 Inc. All rights reserved.

© 2009 K12 Inc. All rights reserved.

"I know!" said Tyler. "But anyone with eyes in their head could see the population of our town was growing fast. Something had to be done to get the library up to speed. And the fact that so many people signed my petition proves I wasn't the only one who

---

© 2009 K12 Inc. All rights reserved.

involved. She's pleased that all those people signed your petition and voted for the new library. Well, I'll be a monkey's uncle," he said in shock.

"I never thought I'd hear her admit she made a mistake."

"Maybe she's just trying to get the new library named after her!" said Mom sarcastically. Everyone laughed.

"That sounds about right!" said Dad. "But if anyone's name should go on the new library, it's Tyler's. Without him, we wouldn't be sitting here talking about it."

Tyler blushed. "Oh, come on, Dad. I just happened to be the first one to think of starting a petition. I'm sure someone else would have done it if I hadn't," he said with sincerity.

thought so," he said as he piled pancakes on his plate. "Be an angel and hand me the maple syrup, would you?" he said to his sister, Karen. He looked over at her and gave her a quick wink.

"I read that the new computerized system will really minimize checkout time," said Mom.

"That's right! I read that, too!" exclaimed Karen as she passed the syrup to Tyler. "You can check out books by yourself now. How great is that? No more standing in long lines! Just scan your card and your books, and you are out of there! That's going to be such a popular feature," she said with a big grin on her face. "I can't wait to try it out."

"I heard they've updated a lot of other things, too," said Mom. "For instance,

© 2009 K12 Inc. All rights reserved.

---

more publicity for herself," he scowled. "Personally, I think we should demand her resignation. I remember how she didn't want to spend any money on this new library. She said it wasn't practical, that we should leave well enough alone. Fought it tooth and nail," complained Dad. "She's got some nerve showing up at the opening," he muttered to himself.

"She's the reason I had to start that petition!" Tyler chimed in. "I never thought I'd see her there!" he said, sounding surprised.

"Well, look at this!" said Dad. "According to this article, the mayor admits she was wrong. She even mentions you by name, Tyler! It says here that she now believes the public was right. She says she's glad you got

© 2009 K12 Inc. All rights reserved.

they've replaced all those old videotapes with DVDs. Same thing with the old music tapes—they've all been replaced with CDs. Welcome to the 21st century, Foster City!" Mom said, laughing.

"It's too bad that Mrs. Zimmerman decided to resign as head librarian, though," said Karen wistfully. "She was so helpful. She always knew where to find anything I needed. I'll really miss her," she sighed. "I remember how she used to read stories to the kids every Saturday morning. And she always suggested the best books for summer reading. She was a lot of fun."

"I happened to speak with her just last week," said Dad. "She said it was the right decision. She felt it was time for someone younger to take over. And it

© 2009 K12 Inc. All rights reserved.

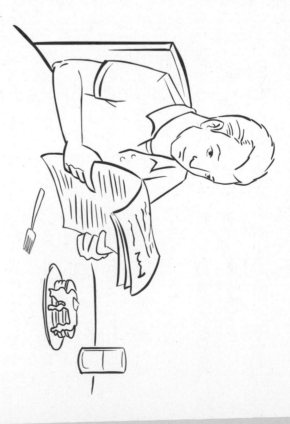

appears that she's really enjoying her retirement. Her rose garden has never looked better!" Dad picked up the newspaper and started to read the front page. "Oh, look! Here's an article about today's opening. I see the mayor will be there. I guess she's looking to drum up

© 2009 K12 Inc. All rights reserved.

Name:

Unit 13 Assessment

Part 1.

Listen to each word that is read to you. Write each word on the lines provided.

1. _____

2. _____

3. _____

4. _____

5. _____

6. _____

7. _____

8. _____

9. _____

10. _____

11. _____

12. _____

13. _____

14. _____

15. _____

© 2009 K12 Inc. All rights reserved.

Word Relationships and Root Words

Part 2.

Read each definition below. Underline the correct root word in the second line that matches each definition.

16. Definition: free

   Root words: astro, cert, cline, domus, liber, mand, min, nov

17. Definition: to lean

   Root words: astro, cert, cline, domus, liber, mand, min, nov

18. Definition: sure or definite

   Root words: astro, cert, cline, domus, liber, mand, min, nov

19. Definition: star

   Root words: astro, cert, cline, domus, liber, mand, min, nov

20. Definition: house

   Root words: astro, cert, cline, domus, liber, mand, min, nov

21. Definition: order

   Root words: astro, cert, cline, domus, liber, mand, min, nov

22. Definition: small

   Root words: astro, cert, cline, domus, liber, mand, min, nov

23. Definition: new

   Root words: astro, cert, cline, domus, liber, mand, min, nov

© 2009 K12 Inc. All rights reserved.

Part 3.

Choose the word from the box that best matches each definition. Write that word on the line provided.

certain	command	domicile	renovate
liberty	minimum	recline	astronomer

24. Definition: a person's home

Answer: _____

25. Definition: an order or direction

Answer: _____

26. Definition: to lie down or lean back

Answer: _____

27. Definition: sure or without question

Answer: _____

28. Definition: to restore or make like new

Answer: _____

29. Definition: one who studies the stars and other heavenly bodies

Answer: _____

30. Definition: the condition of being free from the control of others

Answer: _____

31. Definition: the smallest amount or number that is possible or allowed

Answer: _____

© 2009 K12 Inc. All rights reserved.

Part 4.

Choose the word from the box that best completes each sentence. Write each word on the lines provided.

astronaut	certificate	decline	demand
domestic	liberate	minus	novelty

32. Fifteen _____ five equals ten.

33. As people age, there is a _____ in their strength.

34. I am researching the history of _____ cats.

35. The _____ wore a space suit for protection.

36. The automobile was a _____ when it was first invented.

I received a _____ for volunteering at the animal shelter.

_____ to speak with a manager!" the unhappy customer

3. _____ as about an army on a mission to _____

_____ prisoner during a war.

© 2009 K12 Inc. All rights reserved.

Get Ready

- A *noun* is a person, a place, or a thing. A *proper noun* names a specific noun, and must be capitalized. A *singular noun* is one noun. A *plural noun* is more than one noun. A *possessive noun* shows ownership, and uses an apostrophe to show possession.

   Dan and his *friends* are going to *Mike's house* in *Springfield*.

- A *verb* is an action word. Verbs must agree with the subject in person and in number. Some verbs are regular, and some verbs are irregular.

   I *am* a fast runner. Jan *is* a fast swimmer. We *are entering* the race.

- *Conjunctions* are connecting words. They are used to form compound sentences, compound subjects, compound predicates, and compound objects. Common conjunctions are *and, or,* and *but*.

   Ann *and* Vicky are not sure whether they are going to the mall *or* the shops downtown, *but* Sara wants to join them.

- Sentences can be *declarative* (a statement), *interrogative* (a question), *imperative* (a command), or *exclamatory* (an excited statement or command).

- The *subject* of a sentence is *who* or *what* the sentence is about. The *predicate* of a sentence tells more about what the subject is or does. The *direct object* of a sentence is a noun or pronoun that completes the action of the verb.

© 2009 K12 Inc. All rights reserved.

Try It

Draw a line from each term on the left to its definition on the right.

1. noun   who or what a sentence is about

2. verb   a person, place, or thing

3. conjunction   tells what the subject is or does

4. subject   an action word

5. predicate   a noun or pronoun that completes the
                       action of the verb

6. direct object   or, and, or but

Read the sentence below. Then answer the questions following the sentence.

The Egyptian pharaoh's daughter will find Moses in the bulrushes and will
help him and his family.

7. What kind of sentence is this? _____

8. What are the verbs? _____

9. What is the subject? _____

10. What are the direct objects? _____

11. What is the proper noun? _____

12. What is the proper adjective? _____

© 2009 K12 Inc. All rights reserved.

MARK¹² Reading III Review

Part 1.

Read each set of three words. Underline the word from each set that contains a long vowel sound.

1. rain, ran, run

2. dream, drum, dim

3. song, snow, sour

4. why, when, who

5. few, far, firm

6. allow, away, awful

7. bad, body, boy

8. match, met, might

9. wagon, window, world

10. napkin, neck, nephew

Part 2.

Listen to each sound as it is read to you. Underline the group or groups of letters that can make each sound.

11. oi   ou   ow   oy   ace   ice

12. oi   ou   ow   oy   ace   ice

13. oi   ou   ow   oy   ace   ice

© 2009 K12 Inc. All rights reserved.

Part 3.

Read each sentence below. Underline *true* if the spelling rule is correct; underline *false* if the spelling rule is incorrect.

14. When a word ends in soft *c*, keep the silent *e* and add *–able*. (true, false)

15. When a word ends in soft *g*, drop the silent *e* and add *–able*. (true, false)

16. Words that end in *–ible* can also end in /shun/. (true, false)

17. When a word ends in silent *e*, keep the *e* and add *–able*. (true, false)

Part 4.

Read each singular noun in the first column. Then write the plural form of each noun in the second column.

Singular	Plural
18. journey	
19. hobby	
20. echo	
21. calf	
22. loaf	
23. potato	
24. library	
25. highway	
26. holiday	
27. county	

© 2009 K12 Inc. All rights reserved.

Part 5.

Combine each base word and vowel suffix listed below. Then write the new words on the lines provided.

28. (stand, –*ing*) _____   33. (fix, –*ed*) _____

29. (step, –*ed*) _____   34. (balance, –*ed*) _____

30. (healthy, –*er*) _____   35. (matter, –*ed*)_____

31. (refer, –*ing*) _____   36. (display, –*ed*) _____

32. (share, –*ed*) _____   37. (box, –*er*) _____

Part 6.

On the lines provided, write the contractions formed by the two words that you are given.

38. they + will = _____   43. will + not = _____

39. what + is = _____   44. she + will = _____

40. you + would = _____   45. has + not = _____

41. should + not =_____   46. have + not = _____

42. let + us = _____   47. I + am = _____

© 2009 K12 Inc. All rights reserved.

Part 7.

Choose the prefix or suffix from the box that matches each definition below. Write that prefix or suffix on the line provided.

–ation	–ist	pre–	re–	un–

48. not _____

49. again _____

50. before _____

51. one who _____

52. state or condition of being _____

Part 8.

Read each definition below. From the choices listed, underline the correct base word that matches the definition.

53. Definition: to do or to behave
Base words: act, deficit, flex, grace, port

54. Definition: to carry
Base words: act, deficit, flex, grace, port

55. Definition: to bend
Base words: act, deficit, flex, grace, port

56. Definition: a charming or attractive manner
Base words: act, deficit, flex, grace, port

57. Definition: a shortage
Base words: act, deficit, flex, grace, port

© 2009 K12 Inc. All rights reserved.

Part 9.

Chose the word from the box that best completes each sentence. Write that word on the line provided.

construction	inspects	prescribe	valuable	victory

58. The antique desk is very _____ .

59. My brother led his baseball team to a _____ .

60. My sister asked her doctor to _____ some medicine for her cold.

61. I volunteered to help with the _____ of the new playground.

62. My father always _____ the eggs for cracks before he puts them in his shopping cart.

© 2009 K12 Inc. All rights reserved.

Capital Letters

© 2009 K12 Inc. All rights reserved.

A B C D E F G H

I J K L M N O P

© 2009 K12 Inc. All rights reserved.

| Q | R | S | T | U | V | W | X |

| Y | Z |

Lowercase Letters

| b | b | b | a | a | a | a |

| e | d | d | d | d | c | c |

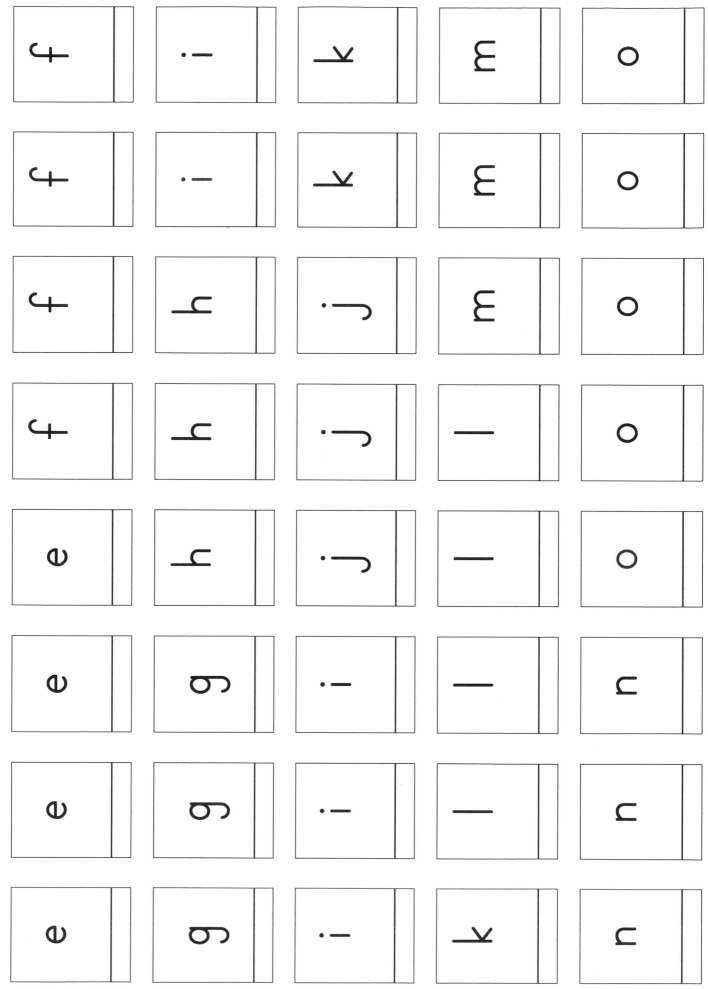

© 2009 K12 Inc. All rights reserved.

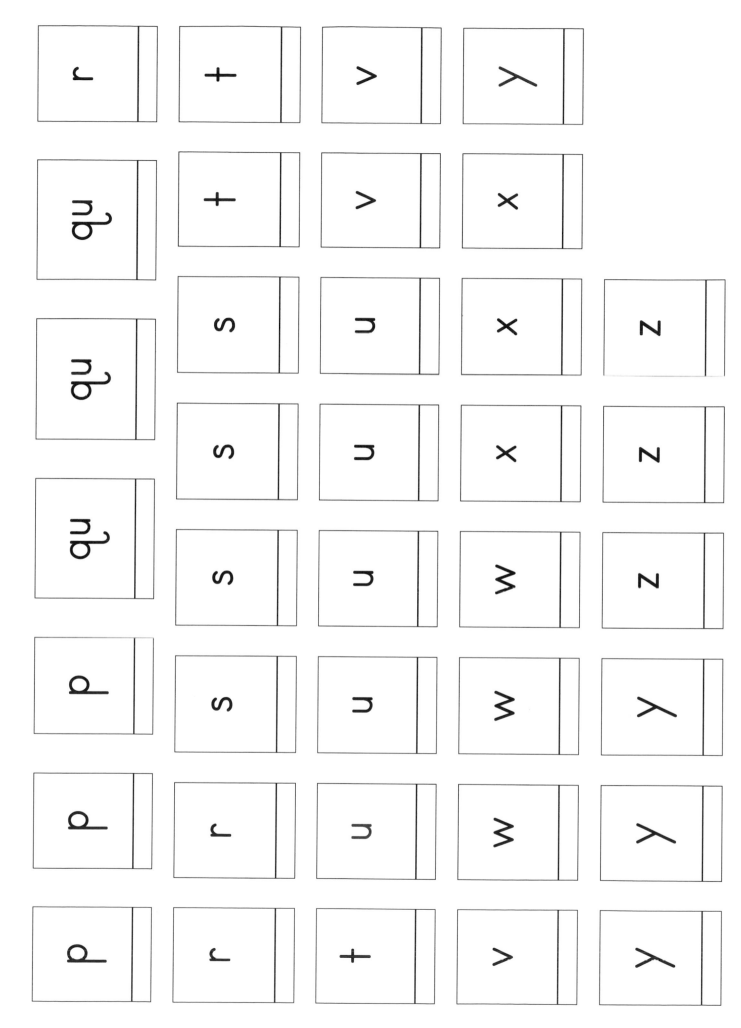

© 2009 K12 Inc. All rights reserved.

© 2009 K12 Inc. All rights reserved.

Punctuation Marks

,	?	!	,	.

Digraphs

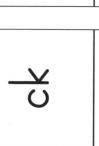
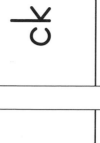
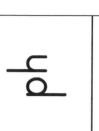
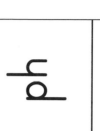

th	ck
th	ck
th	ph
ch	ph
ch	wh
sh	wh
sh	th

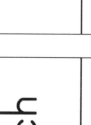
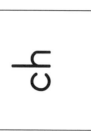

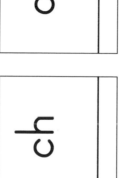

Trigraphs

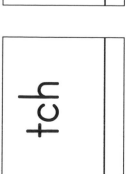
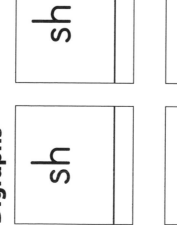

tch
tch

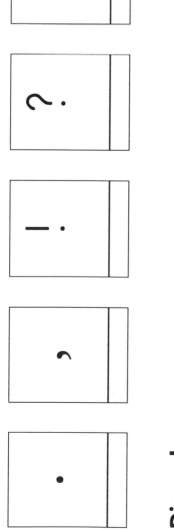
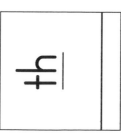
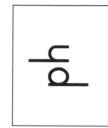

© 2009 K12 Inc. All rights reserved.

Common Word Endings

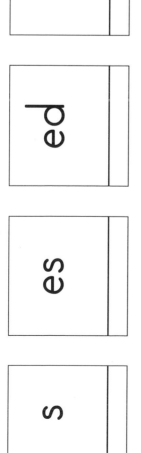

est er ing ed es s

Double Trouble Endings

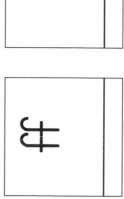

all zz ss ll ff

© 2009 K12 Inc. All rights reserved.

–NG

ng	ang	ing	ong	ung

–NK

nk	ank	ink	onk	unk

/ā/ as in day

a	ai	ay	eigh	a–e	a	e

Unusual spelling for /ā/

ea

© 2009 K12 Inc. All rights reserved.

/ē/ as in me

e-e ey y ie ea ee

e

e e

/ī/ as in hi

e i i-e igh

y ie

e y y-e

© 2009 K12 Inc. All rights reserved.

/ō/ as in no

o

ow

oa

oe

o–e

o

e

ough

/ū/ as in music

u

u–e

u

e

ue

ew

eu

© 2009 K12 Inc. All rights reserved.

/ōō/ as in boot

oo	u	ue	ew	u–e	u

e	ough

/ŏŏ/ as in book

oo	u	ou

/ar/ as in car

ar

/or/ as in for

ar	or	oar	ore

schwa

/e/

© 2009 K12 Inc. All rights reserved.

/er/ as in her

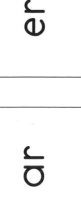 ar    er    ir    or   ur   ear

suffix –ed endings (as in hunted, sailed, and jumped)

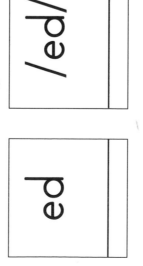 ed   /ed/   /d/   /t/

/f/ as in fit

f   ph   gh

/g/ as in game

g   gu   gh

/j/ as in judge

j   g   dge

© 2009 K12 Inc. All rights reserved.

/k/ as in kick

| k | c | ck | ch | que |

/l/ as in like

| l | le | el | al |

/m/ as in mom

| m | mb | mn |

/n/ as in no

| n | kn | gn | pn |

/r/ as in rat

| r | wr | rh |

/s/ as in sun

| s | c | sc |

/z/ as in zoo

| z | s | x |

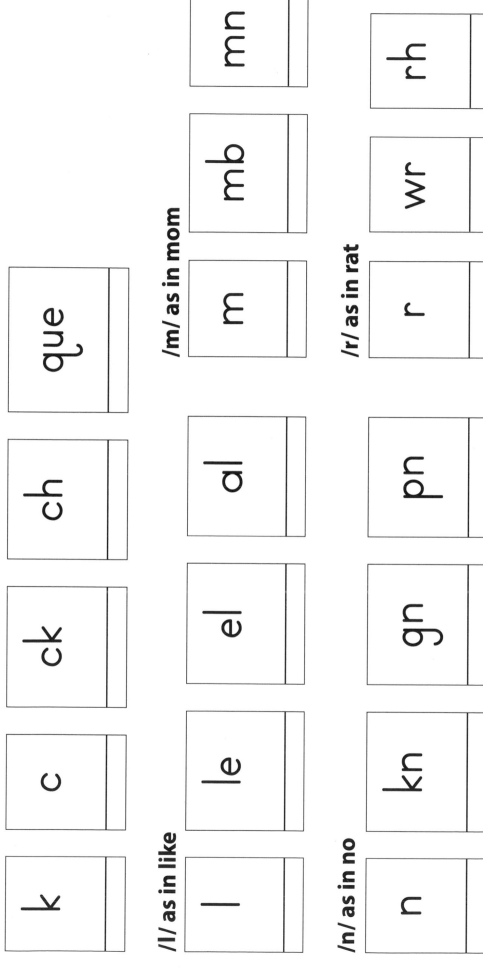